THE *RUDDER* OF THE DAY

*Stories and Scriptures to
Begin the Work Day*

DAN MILLER

*author of **48 Days to the Work You Love***

0-9659072-3-6

Published by Vitology Press,
Franklin, Tennessee

Cover design by Jared Miller
Book design by Charles Sutherland

Subject Headings: MOTIVATIONAL
                  LEADERSHIP

Scripture quotations have been taken from the Holman Christian Standard Bible®, (HCSB) Copyright © 1999, 2000, 2003 by Holman Bible Publishers, (KJV), King James Version of the Bible, (NIV), the Holy Bible, New International Version, © 1973, 1978, 1984 by Inernational Bible Society, and (TLB), the Living Bible, © Tyndale House Publishers, Wheaton, Ill., 1971.

For a free list of all complimentary work/job related products:
http://www.48days.com/products.php

DEDICATION

—∞—

Lovingly dedicated to my wife, Joanne, who has been the main supporting
character in my life story for more than 37 years. My days begin and end
with your prayers, love and unflinching support. God's finest earthly gift
to me is the privilege of knowing and loving you. Your unquestioning
enthusiasm for my many projects has allowed me to explore unknown
territory and achieve levels of success envied by any man.

Thanks for being the faithful and accurate "rudder" in my life.

CONTENTS

INTRODUCTION

H enry Ward Beecher said, "The first hour is the rudder of the day—the Golden Hour." Since I have discovered that principle, I have seen its truth confirmed in many ways.

Be very careful how you start your morning. You are planting the seeds for what the day will hold. If you get up late, grab a cup of coffee and a Twinkie, rush to work fuming at the idiots in traffic, and drop down exhausted at your desk at 8:10, you have set the tone for your day. Everything will seem like pressure and your best efforts will be greatly diluted.

The importance of planting wholesome, life-enriching thoughts in our minds in that first hour of the day cannot be overemphasized. I never read the paper first thing in the morning, no matter how important it may seem to know the news. The news is filled with rape, murder, pestilence, and heartache, and that is not the input I want in my brain. Later in the day, I can scan the news for anything related to my areas of interest and quickly sort through what I need. But I carefully protect that first hour of the day, making sure that all input is positive, clean, pure, creative and inspirational.

These vignettes appeared originally in the **48 Days** newsletter. Starting with 67 names, the list has grown to over 40,000 people who want to start their week with hope and positive inspiration that can bring out their very most productive and fulfilling potential in the workplace.

I am confident the vignettes, the quotations, the related Biblical references and the application to your own life will enrich your daily walk as well. Enjoy the process as you laugh, cry and learn from the life principles relayed in these stories.

And remember this important thought, *"The first hour is the rudder of the day."*

Dan Miller
Franklin, TN

To subscribe to the free **48 Days** weekly newsletter, go to: www.48Days.com

ALL BEGINNINGS ARE HOPEFUL

CREATING A NEW BEGINNING CAN SPARK HOPE, ENTHUSIASM AND CONFIDENCE!

"*All beginnings are hopeful*" is actually a quote from the president of Oxford University, spoken to the entering freshman in 1944, in the midst of a world war. This is a concept that we have seen confirmed throughout history. In working with people going through change, I am often struck by the discouragement, frustration, and frequent anger and resentment. I have come to recognize however, that those feelings always tell me that the person is looking backward, at something that has already occurred. As soon as we are able to create a clear plan for the future, those feelings quickly begin to dissipate and are replaced by hope, optimism and enthusiasm. In all my years of life coaching, I have never seen a person who has clear plans and goals who is also depressed. They just don't go together.

The beginning is always today. —Mary Wollstonecraft Shelley (1797–1851)

Mark came to see me as a frustrated dentist. He described getting into dentistry with no real passion but simply as something that was respected and predictably profitable. He tried to compensate himself for the sacrifices he made there by living a lifestyle beyond his means. Having accumulated over $1 million in personal debt, he now felt trapped from both sides—unfulfilling work and the bondage of debt. It was only as we began the process of identifying new direction and opportunities that hope and optimism began to resurface.

The beginning is the most important part of the work.
—**Plato (427 BC–347 BC), The Republic**

Viktor Frankl, in his wonderful little book, "Man's Search for Meaning", relates his observations of people in the German concentration camps. Age, health, education or ability could not predict those who survived the atrocities there. No, rather it was only those who believed that there was something better coming tomorrow who were able to survive and ultimately walk away from those camps.

Feeling discouraged? Miserable in your job? Just lost your business? Give yourself a new beginning tomorrow! *"All beginnings are hopeful."*

From the end spring new beginnings.　　　　　**—Pliny the Elder (23 AD–79 AD)**

Who could you encourage today? Is there someone who needs the hope of a new beginning?

FROM THE BIBLE:

"Because of the Lord's great love we are not consumed, for his compassions never fail. They are new every morning; great is your faithfulness."

LAMENTATIONS 3: 22-23 (NIV)

DIRECTION FOR TODAY:

In what area of your life can you have a new beginning today?

_____

_____

_____

_____

_____

_____

GET OFF THE NAIL—TODAY

ARE YOU TOLERATING A FAMILIAR PAIN THAT IS PROMPTING YOU TOWARD A NEW AND UNREALIZED OPPORTUNITY?

I heard a story from my friend Bob about an old dog lying on the front porch. A neighbor approached the porch and could hear the dog softly moaning. He asked his friend why the dog was whimpering. And the owner said: "He's lying on a nail." Predictably the man said, "Well, why doesn't he move?" To which the owner replied, "I guess it doesn't hurt quite that much yet."

About a year after sharing this story in my weekly newsletter I had an attorney call me. He said he was that old dog—very much in pain about his daily activities but the pain was still almost tolerable. The image was so indelibly etched in his mind that he started every day identifying with that dog. We discussed his situation, his clear sense that he was off track and the necessity for dramatic change in his life. He was seeing his family, his health, and his peace being eroded by his commitment to keeping things the same. Yet six months later I am still waiting for him to begin the process of introspection and exploration of new options.

> *If you don't have a vision for the future, then your future is threatened to be a repeat of the past.*
> — **A. R. Bernard**

The comfort of familiarity can be so alluring; even if it is not the best. I see countless people droning through their mundane lives, hanging on to their comfortable misery and blocking the thrill of new and unrealized but available successes.

I guess a lot of people are like that old dog. They moan and groan about their situation, but don't do anything. How bad does the pain have to get before you get up and do something else? In the workplace today there are incredible opportunities. If you are in a negative environment, one that causes you pain and anguish, maybe it's time to take a fresh look at yourself, define where you want to be, and develop a clear plan of action for getting there.

"He who has learning without imagination has feet but no wings."
—**Stanley Goldstein**

For tips on how to take advantage of new opportunities, check out other information at: www.48Days.com

---

FROM THE BIBLE:

"Deliver me from my enemies, my God; protect me from those who rise up against me. . . . they return at evening, snarling like dogs and prowling around the city. They scavenge for food; they growl if they are not satisfied. But I will sing of Your strength and will joyfully proclaim Your faithful love in the morning. For you have been a stronghold for me, a refuge in my day of trouble."

PSALM 59: 1, 14-16 (HSCB)

DIRECTION FOR TODAY:

What is that familiar but annoying nail that's sticking you daily? What could you do to get up and move?

_____

_____

_____

_____

_____

_____

_____

The Security of Imprisonment

The comfort of familiarity may be keeping you from new and brighter opportunities.

Charles Dickens wrote about a man who had been in prison for many years. Obviously this man longed for freedom from his dungeon of despair and hopelessness. Finally, the day of his liberation arrived. He was led from his gloomy cell into the bright and beautiful and free world. He momentarily gazed into the sunlight, then turned and walked back to his cell. He had become so comfortable with confinement that the thought of freedom was overwhelming. For him, the chains and darkness were a predictable security.

For many people change is frightening. The sameness and predictability of what we have may be more comfortable than the uncertainty of change. Day after day I hear stories from clients about the feeling of being trapped in their jobs and lives. And yet, the comfort of at least knowing what is coming each day appears to be more attractive than the uncertainty of initiating change.

Many people have the "dream" of having their own business. I hear stories about people who purchased a business opportunity, got into a Multi-Level Marketing program, or opened their own antique shop. Six months later they are begging to get their old job back. The challenges of being more independent, having to make decisions about inventory, managing employees, and dealing with new tax reporting forms have caused them to long for the old days—back in Egypt.

Remember those people? When the children of Israel left Egypt they were headed for the Promised Land. But a few days of passing through the desert (a necessary passage to the Promised Land) left them whining to go back to the familiar misery of slavery under the Pharaoh. Yet going through "the desert" is an integral part of getting to any Promised Land. Most business people go through 3-4 ideas and "failures" before they reach extraordinary success.

The first step in creating positive change is to identify what you want. What would the ideal job be? What kind of people would you be working with? What skills would you be using? How would it make a difference in the world? Fortunately, you are not trapped in your job or life. You can choose to walk into new freedom—or you can choose to stay in your own private prison. Like the man in Dickens' story, it's tempting to become "secure" even in negative situations. Yet freedom comes only to those who are willing to surrender the security of imprisonment.

You can't sail to new lands unless you're willing to lose sight of the shore.

FROM THE BIBLE:

"Oh, that we were back in Egypt, they moaned, and that the Lord had killed us there! For there we had plenty to eat. But now you have brought us into this wilderness to kill us with starvation. Then the Lord said to Moses, Look, I'm going to rain down food from heaven for them. Everyone can go out each day and gather as much food as he needs."

EXODUS 16: 3-4 (TLB)

DIRECTION FOR TODAY:

Do you have a secure prison that is protecting you, but perhaps keeping you from a new freedom?

_____

_____

_____

_____

DIVINE DISCONTENT

DON'T IGNORE A SUBTLE SENSE OF UNREST. IT MAY BE THE KEY TO FINDING THE WORK AND LIFE YOU LOVE.

Ralph Waldo Emerson talked about this concept—the "divine discontent." It is my belief that authentic vocational success is tied to our spiritual well being—the identification of those inner gifts and talents that need to be used for us to feel fulfilled. Now I don't want this to be so "spiritual" that we can't find real application, but work has to provide more than just an income.

I see more and more people who are feeling misplaced, off-track or just the angst of feeling like they are not making a difference. With the desire to do something *"noble"* or *"significant"* they are leaving lucrative positions in that search for more meaning and fulfillment. Often they are looking to discard a financially successful professional career path started on years ago. How does a person redirect from a position or profession seen as highly desirable by others?

Emerson said this: *"I see young men, my townsmen, whose misfortune it is to have inherited farms, houses, barns, cattle, and farming tools; for these are more easily acquired than got rid of. Better if they had been born in the open pasture and suckled by a wolf, that they might have seen with clearer eyes what field they were called to labor in."*

Frequently I see "advantages" given early in life that misdirect a person and leave him/her with a strong desire to change course in their 40s or 50s. The best medical, dental or law schools cannot provide enough benefit to provide a fulfilling career path if that path is not a match with the unique gifts of the person involved. The process of finding authenticity is a very individualized and internal one.

Expecting the government or corporations to provide fulfilling jobs is to reverse the process of finding one's "vocation." A true vocation helps us grow as persons while we meet our own needs and address the needs of those around us. To have someone "give" you a job is likely to short-circuit the process of finding your "calling." Believe you can structure your work around your goals, meaningful relationships, and your dreams and passions. Look inward to give shape to the work that is fitting for you and the application will appear.

Expect change and workplace volatility to enhance your chances of creating meaningful work. I find that it is often in the midst of change that we find our true direction.

Emerson adds: *"A foolish consistency is the hobgoblin of little minds, adored by little statesman and philosophers and divines. With consistency a great soul has simply nothing to do."*

FROM THE BIBLE:

"Happy is the man who finds wisdom and who acquires understanding, for she is more profitable than silver, and her revenue is more profitable than gold."

PROVERBS 3: 13-14 (HCSB)

DIRECTION FOR TODAY:

Can you identify an area of "divine discontent" that is prompting you to make some changes? What can you do to act on that today?

_____

_____

_____

_____

_____

_____

Do you want to be a Butterfly or a Freak

Are struggles always something to avoid or are they a necessary part of growing?

A man found a cocoon of a butterfly. One day a small opening appeared. He sat and watched the butterfly for several hours as it struggled to force its body through that little hole. Then it seemed to stop making any progress. It appeared as if it had gotten as far as it could and it could go no further. So, the man decided to help the butterfly. He took a pair of scissors and snipped off the remaining bit of the cocoon. The butterfly then emerged easily. But, it had a swollen body and small, shriveled wings.

The man continued to watch the butterfly because he expected that, at any moment, the wings would enlarge and expand to be able to support the body, which would contract in time. Neither happened! In fact, the butterfly spent the rest of its life crawling around with a swollen body and shriveled wings. It never was able to fly.

How do we view the struggles in our own lives? Are they always something to be avoided? If we have a child who has used up all his/her money and then wants to go to the movie with friends, what is the most growth producing response from a parent? If a young couple purchased an expensive car and now cannot make the payments, what is the most helpful response? If I can't pay my electric bill, should my church take care of it for me?

"It doesn't matter if you're on the right track; if you're sitting still, you'll get run over."

—Will Rogers

A world class athlete has to go through years of struggle and rigorous daily training to ever be competitive. Any respected musician has spent hours and hours of making mistakes before finding the notes that create a beautiful sound. Can we recognize the valuable training that is taking place in the struggles of our daily lives? The Tartar tribes of central Asia had a certain curse they used against their enemies. It was not that their houses would burn or that they would contract a disease. Rather they would say, *"May you stay in one place forever."* If we don't see the maturing value of our struggles, that could be our fate.

What the man in the opening story above, in his kindness and haste, did not understand, was that the restricting cocoon and the struggle required for the butterfly to get through the tiny opening was God's way of forcing fluid from the body of the butterfly into its wings, so that it would be ready for flight once it achieved its freedom from the cocoon. Sometimes struggles are exactly what we need in our lives. If God allowed us to go through our lives without any obstacles, it would cripple us. We would not be as strong as what we could have been. We could never fly!

FROM THE BIBLE:

"I know your tribulation and poverty, yet you are rich. . . . Don't be afraid of what you are about to suffer. . . . Be faithful until death, and I will give you the crown of life."

REVELATION 2: 9-10 (HCSB)

DIRECTION FOR TODAY:

Can you recall a time when you felt like you wanted relief from a tough situation? Did the struggle teach you something important?

_____

_____

_____

_____

_____

_____

DREAMERS OF THE DAY

YOUR DREAMS MAY BE THE REAL BEGINNINGS OF THE FUTURE YOU WANT.

In *Seven Pillars of Wisdom*, T.E. Lawrence says, *"There are dreamers, but not all human beings dream equally. Some are dreamers of the night, who in the dusty recesses of their mind dream and wake in the morning to find it was just vanity. But the Dreamers of the Day are dangerous people because they act their dreams into reality with open eyes."*

Now there's a clear picture. Dreamers of the Day are dangerous because they *"act their dreams into reality with open eyes."* In today's sophisticated, technological world we often dismiss our night dreams as the result of too much pizza or having too much on our minds when we went to bed. But what about those day dreams? Are they to be dismissed as just random thoughts passing through our brains? Or could they be the seeds of creative problem solutions, great new opportunities and insights waiting to be fulfilled?

"Cherish your visions and your dreams as they are the children of your soul, the blueprints of your ultimate accomplishments." — **Napoleon Hill**

Henry Ford was famous for wanting his employees to spend time thinking and dreaming. Does your employer encourage you to think—and to dream? Have you ever taken a dream and acted it into reality? Where have your best ideas started?

Don't underestimate the value of your literal night dreams as well, for problem solving and creative approaches to your situation. And by all means, keep dreaming during the day. Tap into those recurring thoughts and ideas that have followed you for years.

"All successful men and women are big dreamers. They imagine what

their future could be, ideal in every respect, and then they work every day toward their distant vision, that goal or purpose."   — Brian Tracy

If you can't dream it, it won't likely happen. Success doesn't sneak up on us. It starts as a dream that we combine with a clear plan of action. Become a Dreamer of the Day and watch your success soar.

Nothing happens unless first a dream.   **—Carl Sandburg**

FROM THE BIBLE:

"And the Lord answered me and said, Write the vision, and make it plain upon tables, that he may run that readeth it. For the vision is yet for an appointed time, but at the end it shall speak, and not lie; though it tarry, wait for it; because it will surely come, it will not tarry."

HABAKKUK 2: 2 (KJV)

DIRECTION FOR TODAY:

What is a recurring dream that you have had? Could it be the seed for a direction God wants you to move into?

_____

_____

_____

_____

_____

_____

_____

BEAT THE JOB-LOSS BLUES

WE CAN'T CONTROL CIRCUMSTANCES, BUT WE CAN CONTROL OUR RESPONSES!

No matter how it happens, a job loss is painful. Maybe you were caught up in a corporate downsizing, and it's nothing personal. Maybe it was personal; your boss was an insensitive jerk who didn't recognize your talent. Either way, it's easy to start questioning your self-worth at such a time. You may wonder if you'll end up homeless, never to contribute in a meaningful way to civilization again. In 30 days, your savings will be depleted. Are your old office workers laughing behind your back? Are your neighbors looking at "the loser" when they see you at home on a weekday?

Well, don't get caught up in the negatives. This will only sabotage your immediate future. Here are some tips for moving forward:

Release Your Anger. It's OK to be angry at the unfairness of the boss, the company or the world. But don't stay there. While you may have been treated unfairly, sharing that will only make potential new employers uneasy and prevent them from wanting you on their team.

Evaluate Your Life. Take advantage of these transitions to take a fresh look at your life. What is unique about you? How important is time flexibility? What income do you want? See this as a time to move up and forward; not down.

Network Constantly. Start each day with an action plan. Get out there and meet people. Talk to anyone you can who might offer suggestions on how to improve your job search. Don't be embarrassed to let people know you are looking for work. You are selling a product, and that product is YOU.

Don't Make Excuses. You are not too old, too short or missing a degree. Excuses tend to become self-fulfilling after a while, and mentally you can become your own worst enemy in the job-search process.

Stay Balanced. Our success tends to spiral up or down together. Career success leads to financial success, more social and family success, etc. The opposite is also true. Don't allow a job loss to turn you into a couch potato. Stay sharp physically and mentally. Keep developing your important relationships.

For more on how to handle a job loss or change: http://www.48days.ibelieve.com/

FROM THE BIBLE:

"The Lord is my shepherd; I shall not want. He maketh me to lie down in green pastures: he leadeth me beside the still waters. He restoreth my soul: he leadeth me in the path of righteousness for his name's sake. Yea, though I walk through the valley of the shadow of death, I will fear no evil: for thou art with me; thy rod and thy staff they comfort me. Thou preparest a table before me in the presence of mine enemies: thou anointest my head with oil; my cup runneth over. Surely goodness and mercy shall follow me all the days of my life: and I will dwell in the house of the Lord forever."

PSALM 23 (KJV)

DIRECTION FOR TODAY:

What is one thing you can do in each of these five areas today?

_____

_____

_____

_____

_____

_____

_____

_____

Work Six Weeks a Year

Is getting more "stuff" always a reasonable goal?

Henry David Thoreau spent the better part of his life writing about man's attempt to find truth and meaning through simplified living. At some point he discovered he could live within the harmony and beauty of nature with a clear conscience and only work six weeks a year to support his lifestyle.

Henry found it difficult to find a teaching job that matched his style so he worked briefly in his father's pencil factory. At age 28, Thoreau built a small house on Waldon Pond and began to devote his time to his writing. Advocating the simple life, his *"Walden"* journey began with: *"I went to the woods because I wished to live deliberately. . . ."*

"And in the end, it's not the years in your life that count.
It's the life in your years."   **— Abraham Lincoln**

This does not describe the typical journey of a college graduate today. Rather, the expectation is an immediate six figure income and the lifestyle that accompanies "success." We live in a society that embraces indulgent consumption as a visible status symbol. The fabulous house tells everyone you have arrived, even if it takes two incomes and being trapped in an unfulfilling job to make it work. The house then sets the expectations for the country club membership, private schools for the children and attendance at the right social events. We work longer hours to pay for the new "stuff" and then have less time to enjoy it. We plead with God to bless us, but the only relief from the self-imposed pressure would be to win the lottery.

Where do we draw the line on consumption if we can *"afford"* the extras? Do you really need all the house you *"qualify"* for? Should we really *thank God* for providing when we finance a car purchase equal to an annual income? Is a vacation in the Caribbean that much more satisfying than spending a week on a needy Indian reservation? Is it truly God's will that we buy into the bondage of debt? How can we give generously when payments are overdue?

Perhaps we, like Thoreau, could take time to savor the beauty of nature around us and to smell the fresh roses of everyday life. *"Simplify, simplify."* *"I went to the woods because I wished to live deliberately, to front only the essential facts of life, and see if I could not learn what it had to teach, and not, when I came to die, discover that I had not lived."*

FROM THE BIBLE:

"Give me neither poverty nor riches! Give me just enough to satisfy my needs! For if I grow rich, I may become content without God. And if I am too poor, I may steal, and thus insult God's holy name."

PROVERBS 30:8-9 (TLB)

DIRECTION FOR TODAY:

What would your life look like if you really had a simple life?

_____

_____

_____

_____

_____

_____

_____

_____

_____

_____

IT'S OK TO FAIL

WHAT WE SEE AS FAILURE MAY ACTUALLY BE PROGRESS.

Thomas Edison was an inquisitive child at an early age. He attended school for only three months where the teacher labeled him as "too stupid to learn anything," quite possibly because of his early hearing problems. His mother removed him from school and decided to teach him at home. She encouraged him to read and he quickly developed a great interest in science, especially chemistry. At 10, he set up a small laboratory in the basement of the family home. At the age of 20, Edison set up a laboratory in Menlo Park, New Jersey where he spent his time as a full-time inventor.

Within two years, he had 40 different projects going and was applying for over 400 patents a year. In 1878, he boldly announced to the world that he would invent an inexpensive electric light that would replace the gas light. Often ridiculed, Edison tried over ten thousand different experiments before he finally demonstrated the first working light bulb on October 21, 1879. When a reporter asked, *"How did it feel to fail 10,000 times?"* Edison replied, *"I didn't fail 10,000 times. The light bulb was an invention with 10,000 steps."*

Who could ever imagine where we might be today if Thomas Edison had not persevered after ten thousand failures? It's OK to fail. From every failure comes the seed of an even greater possible success. Robert Schuller compares this process to a high jumper approaching the bar. If he/she always clears the bar, we really don't know how high that person can jump. It's only when they trip the bar that we have a true measure of their success. Without failure, we can never grow to our full potential. Rick Patino, the great basketball coach says, *"Failure is the fertilizer for success."* Embrace failure as a legitimate step in the right direction.

"Restlessness and discontent are the first necessities of progress."

"I have more respect for the fellow with a single idea who gets there than for the fellow with a thousand ideas who does nothing."

—Thomas Edison

16 years ago I got to taste some of that fertilizer for myself. I owned a 4,000 member health club, an auto accessories business and was very involved in our community and church. Then some banking procedures were changed and I found myself in a frightening situation. My businesses were sold at a fraction of their value and I was left with seemingly insurmountable IRS tax bills and supplier invoices. Although advised to declare bankruptcy, I found it impossible to walk away from even my verbal promises. Yes, the return to any real success took much longer than I ever expected. But I am convinced that the journey through that was the training ground for my success today.

FROM THE BIBLE:

"A man's steps are established by the Lord, and He takes pleasure in his way. Though he falls, he will not be overwhelmed, because the Lord holds his hand."

PSALM 37:24 (HCSB)

DIRECTION FOR TODAY:

Describe a time when you persevered through many attempts to ultimate success in that challenge.

_____

_____

_____

_____

_____

_____

HAVE YOU DECIDED TO BE MORE SUCCESSFUL

ARE YOU LIVING AIMLESSLY OR WITH A CLEAR SENSE OF PURPOSE AND DIRECTION?

Often, we have someone call our office about making a change in his or her life. We send information and then hear nothing. Two years later, that person calls and says, "Now I'm ready to really create a plan." What I always wonder is, What did they do for those two years? And usually, when we meet, it confirms my suspicion that they simply continued doing what they had been doing. We know that we all have a tendency toward continuing the status quo. But once you have made a decision, what would cause you to wait? If you said you wanted to be in better shape physically, when would you like to start? If you wanted to do better financially, when would you like to get started? Many times the years go by and I hear people regret that they did not start something earlier.

There is a recently published book titled *"Five Frogs on a Log."* The essence of the book is this: Five frogs were sitting on a log. Four decided to jump off. How many were left? And it goes on to suggest that there were still five frogs on the log. There is a difference between *"deciding"* and *"doing"*.

> **"How wonderful it is that nobody need wait a single moment before starting to improve the world."**
>
> **—Anne Frank**

Now is a great time to be setting your goals for the rest of this year. No matter when you are reading this, now is a great time. There is something magical that happens when you clearly "decide" and begin to "do." Just clarifying where you want to be 5 years from now will start the process toward the fulfillment of that as reality. What an exciting way to start tomorrow, this month and this year!

There is considerable evidence to indicate that expectations of your future do, in fact, tend to create your future. People usually end up pretty much where they expect. It seems reasonable then, to spend some time determining specific, worthwhile expectations that will make your life more meaningful.

"It takes as much time and energy to wish as it does to plan."

—Eleanor Roosevelt

FROM THE BIBLE:

"Be strong and very courageous. . . . Do not let this Book of the Law depart from your mouth; meditate on it day and night, so that you may be careful to do everything written in it. Then you will be prosperous and successful."

JOSHUA 1:8 (NIV)

DIRECTION FOR TODAY:

What three things will you accomplish this week?

_____

_____

_____

_____

_____

_____

_____

_____

_____

_____

Louder Than Words

What you don't say tells a lot about you.

We are seeing an increasing creativity in interviewing today—on both sides. Many interviewers have a favorite question: "Why are manhole covers round? "How many barbers are there in Chicago?" "If you could be an animal, what would it be?" Some interviewers are big on non-verbal clues as we are told that 55% of communication is non-verbal.

J.C. Penney was infamous for taking potential hires out to breakfast. If that person put salt and pepper on their food before tasting it, the interview was over. Mr. Penney believed that this was a person who made decisions before having all the evidence. Jeff O'Dell of August Technology often asks candidates out to lunch—and suggests that they drive. *"How organized someone's car is provides an amazing indicator of how organized the rest of their life is,"* he says. O'Dell believes that the best job candidates not only will have clean cars—*"no Slim-Fast cans or tennis balls rolling around in the backseat"*— but will also excel at the casual conversation in a restaurant. *"It's a way to learn the personal side of things—whether or not they have a family, do they smoke, etc."*—that doesn't come out in the formal interview.

> *"Thus, by their fruit you will recognize them."*
>
> **—Matthew 7: 20 (NIV)**

I also often ask to meet a client for lunch. In watching how they interact with others, how they treat the waitress, and how they attempt to pick up or avoid the check, I learn a lot about that person. Someone who belittles the waiter behind his back is likely to do the same on the job.

Dave Hall doesn't mind making employee candidates a little more nervous than they already are. Hall, a principal at Search Connection, likes to place want ads that list his company's name but not its phone number; he wants only candidates who'll bother to look up the number. When he's not entirely sure about candidates after their interviews, he instructs them to call him to follow up—and then doesn't return their first three calls. He says he's looking for employees who'll persist through a million no-thank-yous in making recruiting calls.

FROM THE BIBLE:

"When words are many, sin is not absent, but he who holds his tongue is wise. The tongue of the righteous is choice silver, but the heart of the wicked is of little value."

PROVERBS 10: 19-20(NIV)

"Words from a wise man's mouth are gracious, but a fool is consumed by his own lips. At the beginning his words are folly; at the end they are wicked madness— and the fool multiplies words."

ECCLESIASTES 10:12-13. (NIV)

DIRECTION FOR TODAY:

What message would your life send to those around you today even if you didn't open your mouth?

_____

_____

_____

_____

_____

_____

If It Ain't Broke, Break It

FAMILIARITY MAY BE KEEPING YOU FROM PROGRESSING TOWARD A BETTER LIFE.

While this phrase may violate your English grammar, it embraces what we know about today's work environment. Doing things like they were done 20 years ago is very dangerous. As a matter of fact, Peter Drucker, the brilliant business thinker, says that if you are doing things the same way as you were even one year ago, you are probably being left behind. Such is the speed of change in the workplace today.

Here are some recent quotes I have heard from clients:

"I've wasted many years of my life."

"I got too comfortable."

"I'm suffering from burnout."

"I feel like I'm a box of parts and nothing fits together."

"My job has ruled my life."

"I've been too complacent in my life."

"I'm on a greased slide to Purgatory."

"I feel like I'm stuck in Groundhog Day."

One example of the dangers of sticking to conventional wisdom comes from the change that occurred in football in 1906. Prior to this time, football was a low scoring game of running and kicking. Guys in leather helmets plodded down the field with the "three yards and a cloud of dust" strategy that was common to every team. Then in 1906, the forward pass was legalized, making it possible to gain 40 yards with one throw. During that first season, however, most teams stayed with the tried and true, sticking with the conventional wisdom provided by many years of playing the game.

One team took another approach. St. Louis University's coaches adapted to and utilized this new option in the game and quickly switched to an offense that used the forward pass extensively. That first season they outscored their opponents 402-11!

Seek out ways you can bring new methods and innovation to what you do. You may want to take some courses to keep you at the top of your field. You may want to explore new fields as possibilities for your career. You may see a new opportunity in elder care, telecommunications, mediation, arts and drama, or alternative medicine. Spend an hour in the park. Find something in your life today that ain't broke and break it! Look for ways to experiment with "break it" thinking.

FROM THE BIBLE:

"The wise man looks ahead. The fool attempts to fool himself and won't face the facts."

PROVERBS 14: 8 (TLB)

"Therefore if anyone is in Christ, there is a new creation; old things have passed away, and look, new things have come."

II CORINTHIANS 5: 17 (HCSB)

DIRECTION FOR TODAY:

What one thing can you do today to break out of a predictable habit?

_____

_____

_____

_____

_____

_____

_____

Remember The Sabbath

A day of Sabbath is more than just a spiritual suggestion—it's a necessity for balance and restoration.

In the "busyness" of modern life, I fear we have lost the rhythm between activity and rest. "I am so busy." We say this as a badge of honor, as if our exhaustion were a trophy, and our ability to withstand 70 hour weeks a mark of real character. We convince ourselves that the busier we are, the more we are accomplishing and the more important we must be. But is this really so? Does more activity really mean more accomplishment? To be unavailable to friends and family, to miss the sunsets and the full moons, to blast through all our obligations without time for taking a deep breath—this has become the model of a successful life.

Unfortunately, because we do not rest, we lose our way. Instead of BECOMING more, we are just DOING more. We base our value on what we can do, rather than on who we are. Are you making time for healthy "breathing" in your life? Our technologies make us available 24/7 to the demands of our work—if we allow it. If you exhale without having time to inhale, you will turn blue and pass out.

Embrace Sabbath days and times in your life. Wisdom, peace, creativity and contentment will grow in those times. Take a walk, give thanks for simple things, bless your children, take a bath with music and candles, turn off the telephone, pager, TV and computer—carve out those times for restoration and spiritual breathing.

Recently, on a Sunday night we had a violent storm here in Franklin, TN. Our power was out all day Monday. No Internet, no air conditioning, no TV or radio. So my wife Joanne, our son Jared and I spent the day cleaning up trees, talking to the neighbors and going out for lunch. An unexpected Sabbath.

I am fortunate to work in an environment where I see rabbits, guineas, woodpeckers, lightening, clouds, and neighbors. It's difficult for me to find a refreshing pause in the midst of concrete, asphalt and honking horns. My work setting is the result of having a clear goal and a plan of action. I know what works for me. Have you been able to find the work that provides a balance of *"being"* and *"doing?"*

FROM THE BIBLE:

"Remember to observe the Sabbath as a holy day. Six days a week are for your daily duties and your regular work, but the seventh day is a day of Sabbath rest before the Lord your God. On that day you are to do no work of any kind, nor shall your son, daughter, or slaves—whether men or women—or your cattle of your house guests. For in six days the Lord made the heaven, earth, and sea, and everything in them and rested the seventh day; so He blessed the Sabbath day and set it aside for rest."

EXODUS 20: 8-11 (TLB)

DIRECTION FOR TODAY:

How can you unplug your "doing" and enhance your "being" today?

_____

_____

_____

_____

_____

_____

_____

_____

_____

I Was Shocked

Our mind can complete the expectations we have!

Recently I installed three new poles and decorative lights on the driveway approach to our house. Although I enjoy being a handy man, electrical work always makes me nervous. I rented a trencher, dug a narrow ditch and carefully laid the line in the trench. I then proceeded to install the outlets and run the line up each pole before completing the power attachment at our house. Twice in this process I recoiled with the stinging shock of electric power surging through my arms—but wait—there was no power yet attached. I hadn't connected the line to the power source. Just in the "anticipation" of power I was convinced I "felt" it shock me.

I find I'm not alone in this mysterious happening. Commonly known as the Pygmalion Effect, scientists say this phenomenon occurs when *a false definition of the situation evokes a new behavior which makes the original false conception come true.* In other words, once an expectation is set, we tend to act in ways that are consistent with that expectation, even when it's not true.

Whoa—what about expecting a bad performance review, getting fired, being rejected by a friend, believing that all good jobs are going overseas, expecting bad *"luck,"* or *"knowing"* your business is going down the tubes. Could the false anticipation make that event become a reality?

> *"There is nothing either good or bad, but thinking makes it so."*
> **William Shakespeare, Hamlet, Act 2 Scene 2**

Could you reverse the phenomenon? Do you think you could "expect" good things and have more good things happen? Read the current statistics on jobs and business in America—you can find unprecedented growth or the worst employment situation in 30 years.

Yes, I did complete the final hook-up and am now enjoying seeing the actual power surge through the lines to shine in the darkness. I get a little extra enjoyment knowing that I overcame my fear in completing the task. Those lights are a daily reminder that sometimes when I feel a *"shock"* it's not reality but just a false expectation—that I can overcome.

FROM THE BIBLE:

"What I feared has come upon me; what I dreaded has happened to me. I have no peace, no quietness; I have no rest, but only turmoil."

JOB 3: 25-26 (NIV)

DIRECTION FOR TODAY:

Describe a time in your life when you "expected" a negative outcome. What happened?

_____

_____

_____

_____

_____

_____

_____

_____

_____

_____

_____

BLACK CRABS—BE ONE AND DIE

BE CAREFUL WHO YOU ALLOW TO INFLUENCE YOUR THINKING AND ACTIONS!

In the book *Rich Dad, Poor Dad*, Robert Kiyosake tells the story of the Hawaiian Black Crabs. If you go down to the beach early in the morning you can find black crabs. If you gather them you can put them in your bucket and continue walking on the beach. Now those crabs start thinking, *"We are bumping around in this little bucket making a lot of noise but going nowhere."*

Eventually, one crab looks up and thinks, *"There's a whole new world up there. If I could just get my foot up over the edge, I could get out, get my freedom and see the world in my own way."* So he stretches up, pushes a little, and sure enough, gets one foot over the edge. But just as he is about to tip the balance and go over the edge —- a crab from the bottom of the bucket reaches up and pulls him back down. Instead of encouraging him and seeing how they could help each other get to freedom one by one, they pull anyone attempting back down into that confining bucket where death will come quickly.

Unfortunately, that's not an uncommon picture of the world in which we live and work. Many of us live around a bunch of Black Crabs, ready to ridicule any new idea we have and just as eager to pull us back down to their level of performance. Small thinkers find it much easier to tell you why something won't work than to help you find a solution. People who feel trapped and are struggling at a low level of success are seldom the ones who will cheer you on to a new endeavor. I have found that one of the key characteristics of successful people is that they hang around people who are already performing at the level at which they want to perform.

> *"An individual has not started living until he can rise above the narrow confines of individualistic concerns to the broader concerns of all humanity."*
> **—Martin Luther King, Jr.**

In *Killers of the Dream*, Lillian Smith wrote, *"We in America—and men across the earth—have trapped ourselves with that word equality, which is inapplicable to the genus man. I wish we would forget it. Stop its use in our country: Let the communists have it. It isn't fit for men who fling their dreams across the skies. It is fit only for a leveling down of mankind."*

There will always be naysayers and whiners; avoid them. Avoid the Black Crabs around you. Find winners and spend time with them!

FROM THE BIBLE:

"Don't make friends with an angry man, and don't be a companion of a hot-tempered man, or you will learn his ways and entangle yourself in a snare."

PROVERBS 22:24-25 (HCSB)

DIRECTION FOR TODAY:

Who are the Black Crabs in your life? How can you avoid them or move on?

_____

_____

_____

_____

_____

_____

_____

_____

Vocation, Career or Job

Are you living out your "calling" or do you just have a job?

These are three words that tend to be used interchangeably - and they shouldn't be. *Vocation* is the most profound of the three, and it must incorporate Calling, Purpose, Mission and Destiny. This is the big picture that many people often never identify for themselves. It's what you're doing in life that makes a difference for you, that builds meaning for you, and that you can look back on in your later years to see the impact you've made on the world.

Stephen Covey, in *Seven Habits of Highly Effective People*, says that we all want *"to live, to love, to learn and to leave a legacy."* Our vocation will leave a legacy. The word *"vocation"* comes from the Latin *"vocare,"* which means, *"to call"*. It suggests that you are listening for something that is calling out to you, something that is particular to you. A calling is something you have to listen for.

If one looks at the derivations of the words *"vocation"* and *"career"* you will immediately get a feel for the difference between them. *"Career"* comes originally from the Latin word for cart and later from the Middle French word for racetrack. Webster's dictionary defines *career* as *"to run or move at full speed, rush wildly."* In other words, you can go around and around really fast for a long time but never get anywhere. That is why in today's volatile work environment, even professionals with careers like physician, attorney, CPA, dentist and engineer may choose to get off the expected track and choose another career. A career is a line of work, but it's not necessarily the only way to fulfill your calling. You can have different careers at different points in your life.

Job is the most specific and immediate of the three terms. It has to do with one's daily activities that produce income or a paycheck. The dictionary defines *"job"* as *"a lump portion, a task, chore or duty."* In today's rapidly changing workplace, the average job is 3.2 years in length, meaning the average person just entering the workplace will have 14-16 different jobs in his/her working lifetime. Thus the job surely cannot be the critical definition of one's vocation or calling.

Ideally, your *career* will be a subset of your *vocation*, and your *job* will be a subset of your *career*. As an example, if part of your *vocation* is to help reduce pain and suffering in the world, you may choose being a nurse as your *career*. There are plenty of *jobs* for nurses. Thus losing a *job* should never change your *"calling."* If you are off track in your *job*, simply go back to your *"vocation"* to get ideas for a new application of that *"vocation."*

FROM THE BIBLE:

"I . . . urge you to walk worthy of the calling you have received, with all humility and gentleness, with patience, accepting one another in love, diligently keeping the unity of the Spirit with the peace that binds us. There is one body and one Spirit, just as you were called to one hope at your calling."

EPHESIANS 4:3 (HCSB)

DIRECTION FOR TODAY:

Do you know your "Calling" or are you just working a "job?"

_____

_____

_____

_____

_____

_____

_____

_____

Sew Up Your Buttonholes

Maybe you need to brush your teeth with your left hand today!

This comes from a story I read in the classic little book *I Dare You.* A professor once hit upon a great discovery while buttoning up his vest. Or rather, he hit upon the discovery because his vest wouldn't button up. His little daughter had sewn up some of the buttonholes by mistake. His fingers were going along as usual in their most intricate operations of buttoning a button, when something happened. A button wouldn't button.

His fingers fumbled helplessly for a moment, then sent out a call for help. **His mind woke up.** The eyes looked down . . . a new idea was born, or rather a new understanding of an old idea. What the professor had discovered was that fingers can remember. You know how automatic things can become, riding a bicycle, using a keyboard, or even driving home from the office.

Then the professor began playing pranks on his classes, and he found that the answer was always the same. *As long as they could keep on doing the things they had always done, their minds wouldn't work.* It was only when he figuratively sewed up their buttonholes, stole their notebooks, locked the doors, upset their routine, that any thinking was done.

> *"A lot of what we think of as neurosis in this country is simply people who are unhappy because they're not using their creative resources."*
> **—Julia Cameron**

So he came to the great, and now generally accepted, conclusion that the mind of man is "an emergency organ." That it relegates everything possible to automatic functions as long as it is able, and that it is only when the old order of things won't work any longer that it gets on the job and starts working. Keeping things the same may be keeping you stupid.

So my advice is this: ***Sew up some buttonholes in your life.*** Drive a different route home from work. Read a book you would not normally read. Write your name with the hand opposite your normal dominance to see how it wakes up your brain. Take time to stop to help a stranded motorist. Volunteer to help on a community project. And welcome the unexpected *"closed buttonholes"* this week. You may be surprised at having your brain turn on. Who knows what creative ideas or solutions you may discover. You may even brighten up your face!

> *"Research shows that 90 percent of five-year olds are creative, but only 2 percent of adults are."*
>
> —Lee Lilber

FROM THE BIBLE:

"Who is like the wise man? Who knows the explanation of things? Wisdom brightens a man's face and changes its hard appearance."

ECCLESIASTES 8: 1 (NIV)

DIRECTION FOR TODAY:

What could you do today to wake up your mind?

_____

_____

_____

_____

_____

_____

Yes You . . . Read a Book

Here's the quickest way to change the results you're now getting!

I've been telling people for years that the average American reads less than one book per year. It's now a known fact that one half of the students who graduate from college never read another book. With rapid change we are told that even a Ph.D. is obsolete in five years unless the holder continues to read. Reading sweeps the cobwebs away, it increases our power of concentration; it makes us more interesting to be around, and it keeps us abreast of new trends and opportunities.

We are told that you can be an expert on any topic if you read three books on that subject. How difficult is that? If you read just 10 minutes a day, you will read an average book a month. Could you change your success in any area if you read 12 books a year? Absolutely! You could learn a new language, become knowledgeable in history, learn the secrets of direct marketing, double your success in selling, dramatically improve your family relationships, answer your theological questions, or become an expert in alternative healing. Don't allow the slow process of life to be your only teacher. Become a continuous learner.

"The man who never reads will never be read; he who never quotes will never be quoted. He who will not use the thoughts of other men's brains proves he has no brain of his own."

—Charles H. Spurgeon

A college degree is no longer a guarantee of success. Some areas of learning are becoming obsolete in 4-5 years. Computer technology, communications, methods of doing business and even some areas of medicine and finance are changing rapidly. We have been told that you will be the same person five years from now that you are today, except for the people you meet and the books you read.

The man who doesn't read good books has no advantage over the man who can't read them.

—**Mark Twain (1835 - 1910)**

If you are reading this, you are obviously already a great reader. If you have either **48 Days To The Work You Love** or **48 Days To Creative Income**, be sure to look in the Appendix for my suggested reading list. You can transform your success by learning from some of these great books. If you would like an updated list, get the free list at www.48Days.com/resources.php

—∞—

FROM THE BIBLE:

"Get wisdom, get understanding; do not forget my words or swerve from them. Do not forsake wisdom, and she will protect you; love her, and she will watch over you. Wisdom is supreme; therefore get wisdom. Though it cost all you have, get understanding. Esteem her, and she will exalt you; embrace her, and she will honor you."

Proverbs 4: 5-8 (NIV)

DIRECTION FOR TODAY:

What are the three great books that you would like to read in the next three months?

_____

_____

_____

_____

_____

_____

ZEWDIE THE CABBIE

How could you brighten someone's day today?

My wife, Joanne, and I were in Chicago at Christmastime, seeing the lights and celebrating her birthday. Because of the congested traffic and impossible parking, we always use public transportation when in Chicago. I happen to love driving and it's always a challenge to be at the mercy of planes, trains, and taxi-cabs. The last cab ride of the trip returned us from our hotel to the airport. Fortunately, we had a cab driver, Zewdie, who seemed to be in his right mind, an interesting conversationalist and even a courteous driver. This after experiencing several who made kamikaze pilots look like sissies. When I complimented Zewdie about his safe driving, he lit up like a Christmas tree and asked if I would write a letter of commendation, which I gladly agreed to do.

It reminded me how simple it is to brighten someone's day. Who do you know that needs a compliment? Who could you build up and encourage by thanking him/her for a job well done? It's easy to see the incompetence in waiters, clerks, service people and even professionals. But do you take a minute to compliment those who do provide exemplary service? Our mailman often comes back our long lane to hand deliver the frequent packages too large to fit into our mailbox. When we thank him he assures us that he enjoys the break in his routine and that he enjoys doing his job well. I called the owner of our yard maintenance crew recently just to compliment him on the incredible job his guys were doing to make our place look beautiful. He was astounded and told me that most people only call to complain.

> *"Nothing else can quite substitute for a few well-chosen, well-timed, sincere words of praise. They're absolutely free and worth a fortune."*
> — **Sam Walton**

How would your own family members respond to a kind word or compliment today?

No matter what the time of year, we can find opportunities to compliment a friendly smile, a helpful act, or an unusual quality of work. What an easy, inexpensive way to really "make a difference."

"Kindness is the language which the deaf can hear and the blind can see."
— **Mark Twain**

FROM THE BIBLE:

"A word fitly spoken is like apples of gold in pictures of silver."

PROVERBS 25:11 (TLB)

"Since you have been chosen by God who has given you this new kind of life, and because of his deep love and concern for you, you should practice tenderhearted mercy and kindness to others."

COLOSSIANS 4:12 (TLB)

DIRECTION FOR TODAY:

What are three things you could do today to brighten the life of someone you meet?

_____

_____

_____

_____

_____

_____

I Want To Be A Sidewalk Man

Finding God's unique gifts is the path to a fulfilling life.

A recent Saturday was a beautiful day that allowed us to complete some outdoor projects. Joanne and I purposely had our three grandchildren at our house to experience the excitement of the day. A crew was working on forms for a new sidewalk before we woke up. The roofers were here by 7:30 AM. Caleb, my 6-yr. old grandson, was especially fascinated by all the work being completed. The concrete truck arrived and began to dump the concrete in the prepared forms. Intrigued by the big boots and the opportunity to walk around in wet concrete, Caleb quickly informed us that he wanted to be a "sidewalk man" when he grows up. Although he briefly reconsidered when we were sitting on the peak of our roof talking to the roofers, he informed them as well of his intentions. Of course, one of the roofers quickly dismissed his newly formed goal and told him to make sure he gets a desk job.

Finding our purpose or helping a child find theirs is an exciting process. By recognizing our (1) Skills and Abilities, (2) Personality Traits, and (3) Values, Dreams and Passions, we can see the patterns in what God has gifted us for.

> *If a man is called to be a street sweeper, he should sweep streets even as Michelangelo painted or Beethoven composed music or Shakespeare wrote poetry. He should sweep streets so well that all the hosts of heaven and earth will pause to say: Here lived a great street sweeper who did his job well.*
> **—Dr. Martin Luther King, Jr.**

Now I know the grass is always greener on the other side of the fence, and this is just one more example. But I also know that if a person provides a quality skill like creative sidewalk construction, they are not likely to ever be out of work. And we see those cushy "desk jobs" come and go like the wind today. Caleb is growing up in a world where his Daddy, Uncle and Papa are all doing desk jobs. How exciting it is to watch his unique God-given talents develop! I would certainly not want to misdirect him from finding his passion and the application of that. And personally, I really do believe the world could use another great "sidewalk man."

We must allow each individual to find his/her authentic fit. As parents, we must embrace training up a child in the way that he/she is "bent". (Proverbs 22:6)

FROM THE BIBLE:

"And also that every man should eat and drink, and enjoy the good of all his labour, it is the gift of God."

Ecc 3:13 (KJV)

DIRECTION FOR TODAY:

Have you found an authentic application of God's best gifts to you? What could you do to move closer to that perfect fit?

_____

_____

_____

_____

_____

_____

_____

_____

_____

BUT I THOUGHT THE PAINT WAS WET

ARE YOU DOING THINGS BECAUSE THEY MAKE SENSE OR HAVE HABITS TAKEN OVER CONSCIOUS THINKING?

There is a story about Russia in the days of the Czars. In the park of St. Petersburg Winter Palace there was a beautiful lawn, on that lawn a bench, and next to that bench, two guards. Every three hours the guards were changed. Yet no one could explain why these guards were guarding the bench. One day an ambitious young lieutenant was put in charge of the Palace Guard. He started wondering and asking questions. Finally, he found a little old man, the Palace historian.

"Yes," the old man said, *"I remember. During the reign of Peter the Great, 200 years ago, the bench got a fresh coat of paint. The Czar was afraid that the ladies in waiting might get paint on their dresses. So he ordered one guard to watch the bench while the paint dried. The order was never rescinded. Then in 1908, all the guards of the Palace were doubled for fear of a revolution. So the bench has had two guards ever since."**

> ***"If you want to know your past—look into your present conditions.***
> ***If you want to know your future—look into your present actions."***
>
> **—Old Proverb**

Every once in a while it's wise to ask, *"Why am I doing this?"* If your dad always bought Fords, is that enough reason for you to only do that today? If you're still using a typewriter, either you love that little clicking sound or you have missed the development of some easier ways to write. Perhaps you loved the challenge of your new job 20 years ago, but today you're a different person. Is it time to move on? I recently saw a 44-yr-old client who said, *"I'm tired of living my life based on decisions that were made by an 18-yr-old."* Most people evaluate their lives in retrospect; they simply look back from

70 and wonder how they got there. You can put yourself in the driver's seat instantly by really taking a fresh look at the *"why"* of those things you are doing today.

The modern definition of *"insanity"* is to continue doing what you have been doing and yet expecting different results. Are you ignoring years of experience and knowledge only to continue doing what you have always done? If you want different results, you will have to do something different. If the paint dried years ago, move on!

Don't get caught in habits that no longer are productive or reasonable.

* Paul Lee Tan, Th.D., Encyclopedia of 7,700 Illustrations

FROM THE BIBLE:

"Therefore, if anyone is in Christ, he is a new creation; the old has gone, the new has come!

II CORINTHIANS 5:17 (NIV)

DIRECTION FOR TODAY:

What activities are you doing today that are more a result of habits than of well-thought out thinking?

_____

_____

_____

_____

_____

_____

_____

A Man With a Toothache

Is a "toothache" clouding your bigger picture of success and accomplishment?

Sigmund Freud once stated, "A man with a toothache cannot be in love," meaning simply that the attention demanded by the toothache doesn't allow that person to notice anything other than his pain. In working with people going through job change, I often find Freud's principle to be confirmed. I see grown men ignoring their wives, hiding out to avoid seeing their friends, watching too much TV and eating foods that blunt their minds. I see women embarrassed about yet another layoff stop going to church, spend money they do not have, read romance novels rather than inspirational material, and snap at their kids when asked an innocent question. The "pain" of the job loss seems to mask the health, vitality and success they have in other life areas.

> *"Only those who will risk going too far can possibly find out how far one can go."*
> **—T.S. Eliot**

Yes, a crisis will scream for our undivided attention. However, diverting your focus may in fact be part of the solution. A couple of years ago I worked with a young man who had just lost $3.2 million in a business deal. He was totally in the tank financially and in his career. But rather than fretting about that I prescribed that he would go to the YMCA each morning for 2 hours. His intense focus there initiated the vitality and creativity that allowed him to quickly spring back to success financially as well.

Going through an unexpected or unwelcome change in your life provides a great opportunity to take a fresh look at your success in other areas. Make additional deposits of success in your physical well-being. The energy and creativity that can come from a sharp mind and body can generate the very ideas you need at this time. Organize a potluck with a group of your friends—you'll be surprised how many of them are going through a similar experience and providing one dish will cost you no more than eating your own meal. Pick up a great book to read. If you read only 10 minutes a day you can read a new book a month—and that can transform your insight and preparation for new options. Stay connected spiritually. You'll realize that in the scope of eternity, this event is probably a tiny spot on the timeline.

"What a new face courage puts on everything."

—**Ralph Waldo Emerson**

For a free outline for your goals in 7 life areas, go to www.48Days.com/resources.php.

FROM THE BIBLE:
(Think a broken tooth doesn't cripple you?)

"Break the teeth in their mouths, O God: tear out, O Lord, the fangs of the lions! Let them vanish like water that flows away: when they draw the bow, let their arrows be blunted. Like a slug melting away as it moves along, like a stillborn child, may they not see the sun."

PSALM 58: 6-8 (NIV)

DIRECTION FOR TODAY:

What is the toothache in your life that is demanding your undivided attention? How can you continue being "successful" in other areas of your life anyway?

_____

_____

_____

_____

_____

"Sitting" for Ideas

Are you missing your best ideas—maybe you should stop trying so hard!

Henry Ford once said he didn't want executives who had to work all the time. He insisted that those who were always in a flurry of activity at their desks were not being the most productive. He wanted people who would clear their desks, prop their feet up and dream some fresh dreams. His philosophy was that only he who has the luxury of time could originate a creative thought.

Wow! When's the last time your boss told you to quit working and do more dreaming? Unfortunately, our culture glamorizes being under time pressure. Having too much to do with too little time is a badge of *"success."* Or is it?

The Apostle Paul took long walks between cities, using the time to think and talk. Even when shipwrecked, instead of calling in a helicopter to get him to his next gig, he simply used the unexpected time to create with his mind. Andrew Carnegie would go into an empty room for hours at a time as he was *"sitting for ideas."*

Henry David Thoreau wandered through the woods around Walden Pond, recognizing that the free time created fertile ground for original thinking. I grew up on a farm in Ohio where we got up at *"dawn"* and went to bed sometime after *"sunset."* Neighbors had time to sit and talk and got to any appointments "directly," which could be in ten minutes or a couple of hours.

If you are feeling stuck, your solution may not be in doing more, but in taking a break from the *"busyness"* of life. Try a little *"sitting for ideas!"*

"Learn to pause . . . or nothing worthwhile will catch up to you."

—Doug King, Poet

How do you approach finding solutions—or looking for new and creative ideas?

Have you discovered the power of ideas coming to you at unexpected times? While sitting at the beach, on a bicycle ride, while watching the stars, or while sleeping. Keep a pad next to your bed to capture those fresh ideas that emerge after a restful night's sleep.

FROM THE BIBLE:

"How happy is the man who does not follow the advice of the wicked, or take the path of sinners, or join a group of mockers! Instead, his delight is in the Lord's instruction, and he meditates on it day and night. He is like a tree planted beside streams of water that bears its fruit in season and whose leaf does not wither. Whatever he does prospers."

Psalm 1: 1-3 (HSCB)

DIRECTION FOR TODAY:

When have you come up with your best ideas? What were you doing at the time?

_____

_____

_____

_____

_____

_____

_____

_____

_____

_____

WHY EAGLES FLY AND CHICKENS FLUTTER

DON'T LET A SEARCH FOR "SECURITY" LEAD YOU INTO A TRAP!

Once upon a time in the long, long ago the Eagle and The Chicken were very good friends. One day while flying, the Chicken said to the Eagle: *"Let's drop down and get a bite to eat. My stomach is growling."* *"Sounds like a good idea to me,"* replied the Eagle. So the two birds glided down to earth, saw several animals eating, and decided to join them. The Cow was busy eating corn, but noticed that the Eagle and the Chicken were soon sitting on the ground next to her. *"Welcome,"* said the Cow. *"Help yourself to the corn."*

This took the two birds by surprise. They were not accustomed to having other animals share their food quite so readily. *"Why are you willing to share your corn with us?"* asked the Eagle. *"Oh, we have plenty to eat here. Mr. Farmer gives us all we want,"* replied the Cow. With that invitation, the Eagle and The Chicken jumped in and ate their fill. When they finished, the Chicken asked more about Mr. Farmer. *"Well,"* said the Cow, *"he grows all our food. We don't have to work for the food at all."*

"You mean," said the Chicken, *"that Mr. Farmer simply gives you all you want to eat?"* *"That's right,"* said the Cow. *"Not only that, but he gives us a place to live."* The Chicken and the Eagle were shocked! They had always had to search for food and work for shelter.

When it came time to leave, the Chicken and the Eagle began to discuss the situation. *"Maybe we should just stay here,"* said the Chicken. *"We can have all the food we want without working. And that barn over there sure beats those nests we have been building. Besides, I'm getting tired of always having to work for a living."*

"I don't know about all this," said the Eagle. *"It sounds too good to be true. I find it hard to believe that one can get something for nothing. Besides, I kinda like flying high and*

free through the air. And providing for food and shelter isn't so bad. In fact, I find it quite challenging."

Everything went fine for the Chicken. He ate all he wanted. He never worked. But then one day he heard the farmer say to his wife that the preacher was coming to visit the next day and they should have fried chicken for dinner. Hearing that, the Chicken decided it was time to check out and rejoin his good friend Mr. Eagle. But when he attempted to fly he found that he had grown too fat and lazy. Instead of being able to fly, he could only flutter. So the next day the farmer's family and the preacher sat down to fried Chicken.

When you give up the challenges of life in pursuit of "security," you may give up your freedom.

*(I've never been able to identify an author for this story, and have taken the liberty to modify it over the years.)

FROM THE BIBLE:

"A little sleep, a little slumber, a little folding of the hands to rest, and your poverty will come like a robber, your need, like a bandit."

PROVERBS 24: 33-34 (HCSB)

DIRECTION FOR TODAY:

Where in your life has the temptation of "security" led you to a potential trap?

_____

_____

_____

_____

_____

_____

LOW WAGES, LONG HOURS . . .

IS THE QUEST FOR SECURITY KEEPING YOU FROM SEEING NEW AND BETTER OPPORTUNITIES?

*"M*en wanted for hazardous journey. Low wages, long hours. . . ."* This ad was placed in the early 1900s by the explorer Ernest Shackleton as he was looking for men to help him discover the South Pole. The ad drew over 5,000 brave candidates.

> *"Do not follow where the path my lead.*
> *Go instead where there is no path and leave a trail."*
> **—George Bernard Shaw**

Are you looking for a *"safe"* and *"stable"* position today? One that is secure, predictable and non-threatening? Then maybe you're missing the best opportunities. I truly believe that if defeat or failure is not possible, then winning will not be very sweet.

Today I see fresh college graduates holding out for signing bonuses, guaranteed salaries, benefits, pensions and stock options before agreeing to work with a company. What is a *"safe"* and *"stable"* position in today's workplace? General Douglas MacArthur said *"security"* is *"your ability to produce."* Knowing what it is you do well is your only security. It doesn't come from a company, the government or your union.

> *"Life is either a daring adventure or nothing. Security does not exist in nature,*
> *nor do the children of men as a whole experience it.*
> *Avoiding danger is no safer in the long run than exposure."*
> **— Helen Keller**

A missionary society wrote to David Livingston deep in the heart of Africa and asked: *"Have you found a good road to where you are? If so, we want to know how to send other men to help you."* Livingston wrote back: *"If you have men who will come only if they know there is a good road, I don't want them. I want men who will come if there is no road at all."*

In times of volatility, welcome the possibility of positive new change. What you thought was security may have been keeping you from a higher level of success and fulfillment.

FROM THE BIBLE:

"Do not conform any longer to the pattern of this world, but be transformed by the renewing of your mind. Then you will be able to test and approve what God's will is—his good, pleasing and perfect will."

ROMANS 12: 2 (NIV)

DIRECTION FOR TODAY:

Are you forging into new territory or staying on the "proven" road? Where could you strike out for a new adventure?

_____

_____

_____

_____

_____

_____

_____

_____

_____

Time to Strip the Boat

There is a season in every year when boat owners pull their boats out of the water and put them in dry dock. Certainly not what boats are known for, but a necessary process nonetheless. Over time, various forms of debris accumulate on the hull. Foreign particles and parasites attach themselves to the hull, hoping for a free ride, but creating increased resistance to the smooth flow of water and slowing down the boat itself.

We all experience this process of build-up, sometimes in ways that are slow and difficult to detect. Inaccurate beliefs, unhealthy assumptions, lack of pure faith, succumbing to criticisms and feeling defeat may cause us to slow down and limit our effectiveness. We may even become numb to our original values, dreams and passions. A job loss, financial pressure, low self-esteem and feeling stuck can literally stop us from moving forward.

> *"He who cannot endure the bad, will not live to see the good."*
>
> **—Jewish proverb**

Immediately following a recent seminar on following your dreams I had a man approach me with a questioning look in his eyes. He explained that he had been a pharmacist for 17 years—and in that period of time had totally lost touch with his dreams. He is an example of what I call the *"frog in the kettle"* phenomenon. We know that if you drop a frog in hot water, he'll jump back out immediately. But put that frog in lukewarm water, slowly turn up the heat, and he'll cook to death without moving.

Maybe it's time for you to strip the boat. Put yourself in dry dock and commit to removing all the debris that has accumulated on the hull of your life. Take a fresh look at where you are and where you are going. Hopefully you'll uncover those old childlike dreams once again. The vulnerability of stripping down to the hull may feel threatening, but it's not as threatening as continuing to drag along through life with the weight of unfulfilled dreams and the baggage of misdirected activity.

Business, relationship, financial and health failures often bring us to this point of weakness. And yet it is there that we have the freshest opportunities for new, invigorating growth. Embrace these times as opportunities for reflection, rest and meditation, confident that on the other side will be renewed strength.

FROM THE BIBLE:

"Now your attitudes and thoughts must all be constantly changing for the better. Yes, you must be a new and different person, holy and good. Clothe yourself with this new nature."

EPHESIANS 4: 23-24 (TLB)

DIRECTION FOR TODAY:

Is there an opportunity you think you may have missed due to barnacles on your hull? How could you still capture that opportunity?

_____

_____

_____

_____

_____

_____

_____

_____

For more on handling change with confidence: http://www.48days.ibelieve.com/

TITHING—A LIFE PRINCIPLE

ARE YOU OVERLOOKING OPPORTUNITIES FOR GIVING IN UNCOMMON WAYS?

I have always believed in the principle of monetary tithing and have experienced the blessings and benefits, both in good times and in bad. But I have also believed in the tithing principle that goes beyond just money. What if you tithed your time—meaning if you work 40-50 hours a week that you then give 4-5 hours of your time in meaningful service? In Biblical times, people tithed the actual products they grew or made; I'm confident that we can be more creative in our tithing today than in just writing checks. Here's an additional concept from Mark Victor Hansen, co-author of the extremely successful *"Chicken Soup for the Soul"* series.

DEDICATE YOURSELF TO IDEA TITHING

Just think what could happen if we all tithed ten percent of our ideas back to the world in ways that would help to create wealth and prosperity for everyone and everything. The possibilities would be extraordinary!

Because we are all unique thinking minds and spirits, each of us has unique capabilities that no one else has or can ever have. If we each decided to create ideas, concepts, plans and solutions, every person and every creature on this planet would benefit.

The great thing about idea tithing is that it's free. It costs us nothing. Once we begin to think of just one idea that would benefit the universe, more ideas will follow. Pretty soon each of us will have hundreds of ideas. And our individual ideas, when told to other individuals, will act as a springboard for their ideas. We will inspire each other.

Begin idea tithing today.

An idea can take nothing and turn it into something.

—**Mark Victor Hansen**

"If you have a penny and I have a penny and we exchange pennies, you still have one cent and I still have one cent. But if you have an idea and I have an idea and we exchange ideas, you now have two ideas and I now have two ideas."

FROM THE BIBLE:

"Bring the whole tithe into the storehouse, that there may be food in my house. Test me in this," says the Lord Almighty, "and see if I will not throw open the floodgates of heaven and pour out so much blessing that you will not have room enough for it. I will prevent pests from devouring your crops, and the vines in your fields will not cast their fruit," says the Lord Almighty. "Then all the nations will call you blessed, for yours will be a delightful land," says the Lord Almighty.

MALACHI 3: 10-12 (NIV)

DIRECTION FOR TODAY:

What could you tithe from your life today—other than just money?

_____

_____

_____

_____

_____

_____

_____

_____

_____

_____

THE "RUDDER OF THE DAY"

HOW ARE YOU SETTING THE DIRECTION FOR YOUR DAY?

Henry Ward Beecher said, **"The first hour is the rudder of the day**
— The Golden Hour"

Be very careful how you start your morning. You are planting the seeds for what the day will hold. If you get up late, grab a cup of coffee and a cigarette, rush to work fuming at the idiots in traffic, and drop down exhausted at your desk at 8:10, you have set the tone for your day. Everything will seem like pressure and your best efforts will be greatly diluted.

However, if you get up leisurely after a completely restful night's sleep, you can choose a different beginning. I have not used an alarm clock for the last 25 years, because I go to bed at a reasonable time and have clearly in my mind when I want to start the next day. I get up, spend 30 minutes in meditative and devotional reading, and then go to my workout area. While working out physically, I take advantage of my extensive tape library, so that I fill that 45 minutes with physical exertion combined with mental input and expansion. The motivation of Earl Nightingale, Zig Ziglar, Brian Tracy, Kenneth Blanchard, Jay Abraham, and Denis Waitely, the philosophy of Aristotle and Plato, the theology of Robert Schuller, Dietrick Bonhoeffer, and John Maxwell are the first input into my brain each morning.

"Consult not your fears but your hopes and your dreams. Think not
about your frustrations, but about your unfulfilled potential.
Concern yourself not with what you tried and failed in, but with
what it is still possible for you to do."

—Pope John XXIII

I never read the paper first thing in the morning, no matter how important it may seem to know the news. The news is filled with rape, murder, pestilence, and heartache, and that is not the input I want in my brain. Later in the day, I can scan the news for anything related to my areas of interest and quickly sort through what I need. But I carefully protect that first hour of the day, making sure that all input is positive, clean, pure, creative and inspirational. Many of my most creative ideas have come from this protected time of the day, often when I am in a full sweat. By 9:00 A.M. I am invigorated, motivated and ready to face anything the day may bring.

Just remember this important thought, "The first hour is the rudder of the day."

FROM THE BIBLE:

"Listen to my words, Lord; consider my sighing. Pay attention to the sound of my cry, my King and my God, for I pray to You. At daybreak, Lord, You hear my voice; at daybreak I plead my case to You and watch expectantly."

PSALM 5: 1-3 (HCSB)

DIRECTION FOR TODAY:

What can you do today to set the direction in a positive way?

_____

_____

_____

_____

_____

_____

_____

_____

The Rat Race — Think Like A Rat

You may be able to improve your life if you think like a rat!

We talk about "being in the rat race," but this is probably unfair. It's actually demeaning to the rats. Rats won't stay in a race when it's obvious there's no cheese. The popular little book, *"Who Moved My Cheese,"* showed how even smart rats quickly look for new routes to follow when the cheese is gone. Humans, on the other hand, seem to often get themselves into traps from which they never escape. Some research shows that up to 70 percent of white-collar workers are unhappy with their jobs—ironically, they are also spending more and more time working.

Jan Halper, a Palo Alto psychologist, has spent ten years exploring the careers and emotions of over 4000 male executives. He found that 58 percent of those in middle management felt they had wasted many years of their lives struggling to achieve their goals. They were bitter about the many sacrifices they had made during those years.

> *"A man had better starve at once than lose his innocence
> in the process of getting his bread."*
>
> **—Henry David Thoreau**

Each week I talk to individuals who feel trapped in their current work. They talk about being demeaned, belittled, and emotionally abused. And yet they stay; hoping against all odds that things will magically improve. Some seem to take a martyr's attitude that God is working something out or that Satan is mercilessly attacking them.

> *There is the risk you cannot afford to take, and there is the risk you cannot
> afford not to take.*
>
> **—Peter Drucker**

Rats, however, move on once they realize the cheese is gone or perhaps was never there. Rats would probably be embarrassed to be labeled *"being in the human race"* for doing ridiculous things like continuing to go to a job that they hated every day. Take action to move toward whatever is pure, good and honorable—in your life and in your work.

FROM THE BIBLE:

"You are living a brand new kind of life that is continually learning more and more of what is right, and trying constantly to be more and more like Christ who created this new life within you."

COLOSSIANS 3: 10 (TLB)

DIRECTION FOR TODAY:

Can you think like a rat today? What is an area in your life where you need to walk away and seek a more peaceful solution?

Sometimes You Gotta Let Go of the Peanuts

Keeping things the same may not be a desirable plan.

George has been with the same company for 23 years. He hates his job, changing in and out of his easily identified uniform at the office to avoid having his neighbors identify him in that role. He has missed much of his children's lives, works on his wife's day off, and his health is deteriorating. He is knowledgeable in computer programming and friends frequently ask him about setting up their home and business systems. But he can't imagine leaving the *"security"* of his job.

"We cannot discover new oceans until we have the courage to lose sight of the shore."
— **Muriel Chen**

Now let me tell you how they catch monkeys in Africa. The natives take a coconut and cut one end off to make a small hole just large enough for a monkey's hand to enter. The other end of the coconut is attached to a long rope. They then carve out the inside of the coconut and put a few peanuts inside. They place the coconut in a clearing and hide in the trees with the end of the rope. The monkeys come around, smell the peanuts and reach inside to grab a fistful. But now, with a fistful, their hand is too large to retract through the small hole. Then the natives yank on the cord and haul that silly monkey to captivity because the monkey will not let go of those few lousy peanuts he thought he wanted.

"Twenty years from now you will be more disappointed by the things that you didn't do than by the ones you did do. So throw off the bowlines. Sail away from the safe harbor. Catch the trade winds in your sails. Explore. Dream. Discover."

—**Mark Twain**

We have idealized sameness as loyalty in the workplace. Loyalty is fine but often is just a camouflage for masking the fear of initiating change. Change can be tough but how much misery should you endure before taking it as a sign to move on. Is this really a "cross to bear" or is it the only way God knows how to get your attention? I frequently see things deteriorate in a work situation to the place where the person gets fired. Then six months later they say, "That's the best thing that ever happened to me." Isn't it reasonable then to question being miserable in the job in the first place? Maybe it's time to let go of the peanuts!

FROM THE BIBLE:

"But one thing I do: forgetting what is behind and reaching forward to what is ahead."

PHILIPPIANS 3:13 (HCSB)

DIRECTION FOR TODAY:

What do you need to let go of today?

_____

_____

_____

_____

_____

_____

_____

_____

_____

_____

THE PYGMALION EFFECT

ARE YOUR EXPECTATIONS PULLING YOU FORWARD OR HOLDING YOU BACK?

Remember the famous experiment called the Pygmalion Effect? Twenty-five grade school teachers were told their students were underachievers from apathetic families. Another twenty-five were told their students were high achievers from supportive families. The test scores of the "underachievers" dropped by 25 points, while the scores of the "overachievers" increased by 50 points. However, the students had been randomly divided into the two groups. All factors were equally distributed; the only difference: the expectations of the teachers.

Wow—how might that apply in our own lives? Expect excellence from your children and you are likely to see it. Expect better things from your spouse and it's likely to happen. Expect more from yourself and you will move to a higher level of success. Expect a better job and it will happen, expect extraordinary results in your business and you will "see" ways to make that happen.

> *"Everyone has it within his power to say, this I am today; that I will be tomorrow."*
>
> — **Louis L'Amour**

People sometimes cringe at being told this principle. We all like to have something or someone to blame for our misfortunes. Circumstances, family history, our spouse, our boss or our "luck" are likely candidates for finger pointing. Start believing that "luck" is when preparation meets opportunity.

> *"I learned this, at least, by my experiment: that if one advances confidently in the direction of his dreams, and endeavors to live the life which he has imagined, he will meet with a success unexpected in common hours. He will put*

some things behind, will pass an invisible boundary; new, universal, and more liberal laws will begin to establish themselves around and within him; or the old laws be expanded, and interpreted in his favor in a more liberal sense, and he will live with the license of a higher order of beings . . . If you have built castles in the air, your work need not be lost; that is where they should be. Now put the foundations under them."

—**Henry David Thoreau**

Don't blame circumstances or the expectations of others for where you are today. Claim your purpose, mission and destiny by creating your own future. Begin to "see" the fulfillment of your dreams by setting clear goals and plans of action.

FROM THE BIBLE:

"For I know the plans I have for you," says the LORD. "They are plans for good and not for disaster, to give you a future and a hope."

JEREMIAH 29:11 (NIV)

DIRECTION FOR TODAY:

Are you where you thought you'd be at this stage of life? Where do you expect to be five years from now?

_____

_____

_____

_____

_____

_____

Tough Love

What we see as punishment may actually be a necessary step toward success.

Within a few seconds after birth, a baby giraffe struggles to its feet. Shortly afterward, however, the mother will knock it over from that first wobbly stance. This process is repeated each time the baby struggles to its feet until the young giraffe has the strength to stand in a firm and unwavering position. What seems like an unkind and cruel act is in fact of vital importance to the survival of the young animal. It is, in fact, an act of love by the mother for its child. For the baby giraffe, the world is a dangerous place and it must quickly learn how to respond to unexpected challenges and get back up on its feet. Now I don't imagine that the baby giraffe welcomes being knocked around or particularly thanks Mom for the experience. I doubt that the little guy understands that there is an important lesson being learned.

Is there perhaps a life principle here that we try to avoid as well? What does *"failure"* teach us? Should we avoid it at all costs? Does failure chip away at our fragile egos and lessen our chances of ultimate success? Is it Satan who causes our failures and God who wants us to always win?

Research shows us that entrepreneurs fail an average of 3.8 times before they finally make it in a business venture. They recognize that three steps forward and two steps backward still have a net result of one step of progress. If you can decide to see your own *"failures"* as a necessary part of your progress, you will separate yourself from the average person and put yourself into the category of potential high achiever.

"Many of life's failures are people who did not realize how close they were to success when they gave up."

—Thomas Edison

Most people try to avoid failure like a bad disease. They cringe at the prospect and may stay in a safe but unchallenging position, an unfulfilling job, a familiar but boring car, at the bottom of the hill as others master the peak.

"Failure is the opportunity to begin again more intelligently."

—**Henry Ford**

Embrace failure as a legitimate step in the right direction. See it as a stepping stone toward the success you want.

FROM THE BIBLE:

"If thou faint in the day of adversity, thy strength is small."

PROVERBS 24:10 (KJV)

DIRECTION FOR TODAY:

Describe a time when you felt you were being "knocked down" only to realize later that the experience saved you or made you wiser.

_____

_____

_____

_____

_____

_____

_____

_____

_____

BEWILDERED — BUT NOT LOST

BE AWARE THAT MANY EXPERIENCES MAY INITIALLY
BRAND YOU AS A "FAILURE."

It's interesting that often those labeled as *"failures"* go on to accomplish unusual success.

Here are some recognizable *"failures:"*

Henry Ford failed and went broke five times before he succeeded.

R. H. Macy failed seven times before his store in New York City caught on.

Daniel Boone was once asked by a reporter if he had ever been lost in the wilderness. Boone thought a moment and then replied, *"No, but I was once bewildered for about three days."*

Michael Jordan was cut from his high school basketball team. He later observed, *"I've failed over and over again in my life. That is why I succeed."*

The first time Jerry Seinfeld walked out on stage at a comedy club as a professional comic, he looked out at the audience, froze, and totally forgot how to talk. He stumbled through *"a minute and a half"* of material and was booed off the stage.

Winston Churchill failed the 6th grade.

Steven Spielberg dropped out of high school in his sophomore year. He was persuaded to come back and placed in a learning disabled class. He lasted a month and dropped out of school forever.

In 1954 the manager of the Grand Ole Opry fired Elvis Presley after one performance. He told Presley, *"You ain't goin' nowhere, son. You ought to go back to drivin' a truck."*

33 publishers rejected the first *Chicken Soup for the Soul*. The authors were repeat-

edly told that no one wanted to read those sappy little stories. Those sappy little stories have now sold over 80 million copies.

Moses *"failed"* at being the prince's son—ran off for 40 years—learned some better relationship skills and came back to deliver an entire nation.

Joseph *"failed"* on several occasions, ended up in prison, and then rose to fame and power.

Don't be like Charlie Brown in how you respond to failure. In one segment, he had just built a beautiful sand castle. As soon as he stood back to admire his masterpiece, it gets flattened by a huge wave. Staring at the now smooth spot where his day's work had been moments before, he says, *"There must be a lesson here, but I don't know what it is."* Learn from your failure. See it as a stepping stone toward the success you ultimately want. Don't accuse God of blocking you—read James 1:2-4.

FROM THE BIBLE:

"Consider it a great joy, my brothers, whenever you experience various trials, knowing that the testing of your faith produces endurance. But endurance must do its complete work, so that you may be mature and complete, lacking nothing."

JAMES 1: 2-4 (HCSB)

DIRECTION FOR TODAY:

Remember a "Joseph" time in your life when you felt like you were banished to prison only to realize later that the experience was an important part of your preparation.

_____

_____

_____

_____

_____

How Much Land Do You Need

In our attempts to always have more, how do we know when enough is enough?

There is a wonderful story by Leo Tolstoy, written in 1886. The much shortened details go something like this: There once was a peasant named Pahom who worked hard and honestly for his family, but had no land of his own. By scrimping and saving, he managed to buy 40 acres of land. He grew his own hay, cut his own trees, and fed his own cattle. Then he heard about land in a neighboring territory where the land was so good that rye grew as high as a horse. Pahom's heart was filled with new desire. So he bought land here and was ten times wealthier than he had been. Then one day a passing merchant told Pahom that he had purchased thirteen thousand acres of rich land for only one thousand rubles. Pahom traveled more than three hundred miles to this rich land to explore for himself. The chief of the land told him the price was always the same: one thousand rubles a day. As much land as you can walk around in a day is yours and the price is one thousand rubles.

The next day Pahom began at daybreak. He walked toward the rising sun, moving quickly through the lush countryside. He sparingly drank his water and ate his bread to keep himself refreshed. Several times he saw areas that he knew would do well and added them to his circle. But now his feet were sore, he was exhausted from the heat, and his legs began to fail. Still he walked on. Now the sun was close to the rim and was about to set but he was also quite near his aim. Just a little more land and he would hurry back to the starting point. He added a small pond and a few trees he knew would add to his wealth and his family would enjoy. He ran on, throwing off his coat, his boots, his flask and his cap. He gathered his last strength and ran on. As he neared the final goal, his legs gave way beneath him, and he fell forward and clasped the goal marker in his hands.

His servant came running up and tried to raise him, but he saw that blood was flow-ing from his mouth. Pahom was dead! His servant picked up a spade and dug a grave long enough for Pahom to lie in. Six feet from his head to his heels was all he needed.

Sometimes our quest for more defies common sense. Guard against being so busy making a living that you end up not having a *life.*

FROM THE BIBLE:

"A rich man's land was very productive. He thought to himself, 'What should I do, since I don't have anywhere to store my crops? I will do this,' he said. 'I'll tear down my barns and build bigger ones, and store all my grain and my goods there. Then I'll say to myself, "You have many goods stored up for many years. Take it easy; eat, drink, and enjoy yourself."' "But God said to him, 'You fool! This very night your life is demanded of you. And the things you have prepared—whose will they be?' "That's how it is with the one who stores up treasure for himself and is not rich toward God."

LUKE 12: 16-21 (HCSB)

DIRECTION FOR TODAY:

Is your desire for more an attempt to help others more or just to accumulate more?

_____

_____

_____

_____

_____

_____

_____

Avon Calling

Is there a new opportunity right under your nose?

The first Avon lady was a man. David H. McConnell was a big city bookseller. In 1892, when the perfume he used to reward loyal customers proved more popular than his paperbacks, he dumped the books and began promoting only the perfumes. McConnell's next smart move was assembling a workforce composed entirely of housewives. In contrast to the then prevalent door-to-door salesmen, Avon ladies made friends with their customers and were not the creepy blue-suede-shoe guys that most people expected to see knocking at their doors. By recognizing his true market and how to best relate to his customers, McConnell made a fortune, and so did many of his Avon ladies.

How many businesses do you know of today that continue to do what they've always done, even in the face of a changing market? If you sell appliances and a WalMart opens next door, you may find a shrinking opportunity to sell appliances but an exploding market to repair and service them.

If every yard you mow has a tree stump that needs to be removed, you may discover that rather than just being one more yard service, you have a unique opportunity in stump removal.

A couple of years ago, I worked with a gentleman who had been selling fabric to major apparel manufacturers. He observed that any flaw in the fabric rolls caused it to be sold for scrap. He quit his *"normal"* job, began buying and cutting the scrap fabric into squares to be used as rags. Body shops, auto dealers, and parts stores demanded his product faster than he could produce it. He got a contract with Dollar General to provide the rags packed in plastic bags. He now employs seven neighborhood women to help him stay ahead of this unique opportunity that was right under his nose.

"There is one thing which gives radiance to everything. It is the idea of something around the corner."

—G. K. Chesterton

Our changing work environment is shrinking many of the old business and work opportunities. Even Avon is finding resistance to the knocking on doors model as more and more people purchase on the Internet. But with every change there is the equal seed of new opportunity. The maker of Levi's was an unsuccessful gold miner who recognized that the other miners needed more durable pants for their digging activities.

FROM THE BIBLE:

"Open my eyes so that I may see wonderful things in Your law. I am a stranger on earth; do not hide Your commands from me."

PSALM 119: 18-19 (HCSB)

DIRECTION FOR TODAY:

Where is the hidden opportunity in the changes being forced on you?

_____

_____

_____

_____

_____

_____

_____

_____

_____

YOU CAN GET ALL A's AND STILL FLUNK LIFE

WE'VE BEEN DUPED BY A MYTH ABOUT WHAT TRADITIONAL
"EDUCATION" WILL GUARANTEE FOR OUR FUTURES.

This is an increasingly common theme. We have been sold a bill of goods in thinking that a degree will guarantee fame and fortune. Recent graduating MBAs are finding a very uncertain job market in an economy that's forced companies to delay hiring plans and maybe not even show up at the campus career fairs. Part of this is a somewhat stagnant business environment and part is that the MBA has lost some of its appeal to the business world.

Several years ago I met with a good looking young man who 19 months prior to seeing me had graduated with his MBA from one of the most prestigious MBA programs in the country. He had sacrificed a great deal of time and money to get the degree, fully confident that there would be a selection of $80K/yr jobs lined up for him. However, in 19 months of heavy interviewing, he had not been offered a position of any kind at any income figure. In working with him, it was quickly apparent that he came across as arrogant, condescending, and egotistical. Fortunately, with the pain of no positive results, he was quite teachable and we were able to change his personal presentation quickly and get the opportunities he had been seeking.

"I have never let my schooling interfere with my education."

—Mark Twain

Several years ago a Yale University study reported that 15% of the reason for a person's success is due to technical skill and knowledge, and 85% of the reason originates from that person's personal skill; attitude, enthusiasm, self-discipline, smile, tone of voice, desire, and ambition.

This is why candidates with the best qualifications on paper frequently do not get the job. But what an opportunity to bypass those with perhaps more experience and better credentials. Take advantage of this insight to make yourself a top candidate. Maximize your "human capital."

The greatest obstacle to discovery is not ignorance — it is the illusion of knowledge.

FROM THE BIBLE:

"Stop fooling yourselves. If you count yourself above average in intelligence, as judged by this world's standards, you had better put this all aside and be a fool rather than let it hold you back from the true wisdom from above. For the wisdom of this world is foolishness to God. As it says in the book of Job, God uses man's own brilliance to trap him; he stumbles over his own 'wisdom' and falls. And again, in the book of Psalms, we are told that the Lord knows full well how the human mind reasons, and how foolish and futile it is."

I Corinthians 3: 18-20 (TLB)

DIRECTION FOR TODAY:

What unique areas of "human capital" do you have? How have you used those for unusual success?

_____

_____

_____

_____

_____

_____

_____

_____

Wilt Thou Be Made Whole

Sometimes there's a comfortable misery in predictable, repeating failure.

There was a pool in Jerusalem near the sheep market that was believed to have special properties. The belief was that every so often, at an unexpected time, an angel would stir the waters, and then whoever managed to jump in first would be healed. In John 5 in the Bible, we read where Jesus was walking by and heard the whining voice of a guy who had been coming there every day for 38 years. Jesus walked up to him and asked, *"Wilt thou be made whole?"* Dude, do you want to get well? The guy was probably offended and thought to himself, *"Of course I do. Haven't I been coming here every day for 38 years?"*

But we know Jesus could see through to the heart. The question was a legitimate one. *"Do you want to get well?"* I suspect that enjoying poor health, hanging around at the pool, receiving other people's sympathy and handouts had become this guy's profession. Of course he had reasons to complain. Can't you see how bad things are? He had probably long since lost any hope of changing his situation and had created his own private little welfare system.

Seeing into his heart Jesus said, *"Get up and walk!"* A little confused by the authority, the guy actually found out he could stand up and walk. Whoa! No more comfort of self-pity, no more sympathy from friends, no more of the predictable familiarity of justified whining and complaining. What do you suppose happened the next morning when this guy's mom and dad suggested he go out and get a job?

How many people do you know who are hiding behind the socially acceptable excuse of having a *"disability"* or *"condition"* or *"loser's limp"* that exempts them from the daily responsibility the rest of us shoulder? *"If I got a job, my disability checks would stop."* *"If it weren't for this pain in my leg, I'd be willing to go to work."* *"I'm suing the company because they fired me after only four days of showing up late."* There's safety in being down and out. The real test and responsibility comes with being healthy and well. Thus the question, *"Wilt thou be made whole?"*

Sometimes I fear we sabotage our own success because the familiarity of the known is more comfortable than the uncertainty of the unknown possibilities. If you were offered the chance for a better future, would you take advantage of it?

FROM THE BIBLE:

"One man was there who had been sick for 38 years. When Jesus saw him lying there and knew he had already been there a long time, He said to him, 'Do you want to get well?' 'Sir,' the sick man answered, 'I don't have a man to put me into the pool when the water is stirred up, but while I'm coming, someone goes down ahead of me.' 'Get up,' Jesus told him, 'pick up your bedroll and walk!' Instantly the man got well, picked up his bedroll, and started to walk."

JOHN 5: 5-9 (HCSB)

DIRECTION FOR TODAY:

Is there any "sickness" that you are hanging on to?

_____

_____

_____

_____

_____

_____

_____

_____

AMISH BUSINESS

WHAT ARE THE DEFINABLE CHARACTERISTICS OF THESE UNIQUE ENTREPRENEURS?

In driving through Holmes County Ohio recently, I was again intrigued by the quantity of businesses operating in that strong Amish area. We watched 18-wheelers turn down tiny gravel roads to get to the various businesses tucked among the back roads. The diminishing number of people directly involved in agriculture has affected even this agrarian group. Reports indicate that in this community, more than half the Amish have left the farms to work in small businesses. According to commerce information, there are about 1,000 Amish microenterprises in this area. Many of these boast annual sales of more than $500,000. Yes, employees are making buggies, harnesses and lumber, but also furniture, modern cabinets, garage doors and cheese. Restaurants, hotels, fitness centers and tourists' sites are flourishing.

This is significant because of the trend toward small businesses and home-based businesses in the general population. Yet, while the national failure rate for small businesses is listed as about 85% in the first 5 years, for these Amish businesses, the failure rate is less than 5%.

How is it possible that these Amish entrepreneurs, despite having only eighth-grade education, many with no technological advancements such as computers or even telephones and electricity, have such an astounding rate of success?

The researchers who have studied this phenomenon have identified 5 basic characteristics of these simple yet successful businesses:

1. An ethic of hard work. Proverbs 10: 4 tells us, "Lazy hands make a man poor, but diligent hands bring wealth."

2. Use of apprenticeships to train young entrepreneurs. We have lost the art of mentoring; Jewish fathers always taught their children a trade or skill. Today we are raising sons and daughters with no identifiable areas of vocational focus.

3. Small scale operations. We are so quick to believe that bigger is better. Often it is just bigger.

4. Frugality and austerity, resulting in low overhead. In these Amish businesses, the owner is usually doing the hands-on work. No fancy offices or boardrooms, just the basic needs. Operating from a home farm, many have no rent or lease expense.

5. Product quality, uniqueness, and value. The United States is known for shoddy workmanship and poor quality. A return to quality is a key to success. People expect Amish workmanship to be quality and they get what they expect.

These amazing results appear to be based on simple, basic principles. Integrity, character, and value do have a lasting and profitable outcome.

FROM THE BIBLE:

"Any enterprise is built by wise planning, becomes strong through common sense, and profits wonderfully by keeping abreast of the facts."

PROVERBS 24: 3-4 (TLB)

DIRECTION FOR TODAY:

What are the ways you can increase these 5 characteristics in your work today?

_____

_____

_____

_____

_____

_____

_____

CALLING OR PROFESSION

We have a myth in our society that the more education one has, the more opportunities or choices one has as well. True, more education may lead to more economic affluence and the ability to purchase more stuff. But I find that more education often narrows rather than broadens the choices about meaningful direction in our lives. When someone has spent ten years getting a medical, dental, or law degree, how can that person discover at 40 that he/she really wants to be an artist or a truck driver?

I grew up in the church—and learned a lot about *vocation* in that setting. But I also saw that fulfilling God's will seemed to be to respond to something external; to the voices of other people rather than listening for my own call. I saw moral and religious demands that expected people to be something they were not and often directed toward an elusive goal that was just out of reach.

I had a startling conversation with my Dad recently. Now 91 years old, Dad lives in a retirement center in Ohio. Dad was the pastor of our local church all my growing up years and a farmer in order to keep food on the table. I always assumed that he had received a mystical and glorious call from God regarding his role as a pastor. When I asked him how he heard God's call, he responded immediately, *"Oh, that wasn't me; that was what other people wanted."* He explained that others had seen him as a teacher and then told him he should take that first position as a pastor. He said he never enjoyed the role but felt obligated to do what others wanted him to do. How sad—trying to do something Godly that was not an authentic *vocation* at all. Perhaps that helps to explain the frustrations I saw along the way.

If we had insight into God's perfect plan and training in understanding our hearts at 18 years of age, all would be well. However, those things seem to come as a result of living life and usually offer new options along the way. It often takes years for our hearts to speak, and when they do, we are often too busy with the daily lives we have created to hear them. There is an old Hasidic tale that has been retold in many forms. It relates to the tendency of many well-meaning people to want to be someone else and the importance of finding our true, unique and worthy self. Rabbi Zusya, when he was an old man, said, *"In the coming world, they will not ask me: 'Why were you not Moses?' Rather, they will ask me: 'Why were you not Zusya?'"*

FROM THE BIBLE:

"Is everyone an apostle? Of course not. Is everyone a preacher? No. Are all teachers? Does everyone have the power to do miracles? Can everyone heal the sick? Of course not. Does God give all of us the ability to speak in languages we've never learned? Can just anyone understand and translate what those are saying who have that gift of foreign speech?
No, but try your best to have the more important of these gifts.'

I CORINTHIANS 12: 29-31 (TLB)

DIRECTION FOR TODAY:

Are you walking in your unique "calling" today, or are you living out the expectations of others?

_____

_____

_____

_____

_____

_____

_____

Just Leave Me Alone

Many people are most creative and productive when they are secluded or left alone.

A common myth in clients that I see is the belief that if they are going to do something creative, innovative or entrepreneurial, they must become the outgoing, hard driving Donald Trump kind of person. Of course, this is often very much the opposite of their natural personality style. What do you think? Is it necessary to become the aggressive extrovert in order to do something exciting, unusual and profitable?

I trust you don't really believe that. The key to success is to find your authenticity and to be true to that. Shakespeare really conveyed a basic truth when he said, *"Know thyself, and to thine own self be true, then thou canst not be false with any man."* If you are an introvert who shudders at the thought of being in front of people, then allow your business or career to embrace that knowledge about yourself. There is no continuum of personal style that forces a person to become more extroverted, talkative, bold and aggressive in the path to success.

Here are some notable, quotable examples:

"Solitude is for me a fount of healing which makes my life worth living. Talking is often torment for me, and I need many days of silence to recover from the futility of words.."

—Carl G. Jung

"I hate crowds and making speeches. I hate facing cameras and having to answer to a crossfire of questions. Why popular fancy should seize upon me, a scientist, dealing in abstract things and happy if left alone, is a manifestation of mass psychology that is beyond me."

—Albert Einstein

"We have to remember that we look for solitude in order to grow there in love for God and in love for others. We do not go into the desert to escape people but to learn how to find them: we do not leave them in order to have nothing more to do with them, but to find out the way to do them the most good."

—Thomas Merton

Silence is not just a void space. Silence is often where God is, waiting to burst forth with the possibility of a creative solution or a miraculous thought. Out of the silence comes the next chapter in a book or the opening chords of a symphony. Out of silence comes the natural breathing rhythm of restful rejuvenation and healthy optimism.

Workaholics and others addicted to frenetic activity miss the life-giving power of silence.

FROM THE BIBLE:

"The quiet words of the wise are more to be heeded than the shouts of a ruler of fools."

Ecclesiastes 9: 17 (NIV)

DIRECTION FOR TODAY:

What are the ways you have violated being "true to thine own self?" How can you tap into the power of silence in your work and life?

_____

_____

_____

_____

_____

_____

SOUL-LESS WORK

IS BUSYNESS CROWDING OUT THE ROOM FOR THE SUCCESS OF YOUR SOUL?

The story is told of a South American tribe that went on a long march, day after day, when all of a sudden they would stop walking, sit down to rest for a while, and then make camp for a couple of days before going any further. They explained that they needed the time of rest so that their souls could catch up with them. (from *"Sabbath"* by Wayne Muller)

Are you working and living without the benefits of having your soul catch up? Are you feeling like your work is soul-less and little more than a method of producing a paycheck?

In the "busyness" of modern life, I fear we have lost the rhythm between activity and rest. Just as exhaling without occasionally inhaling will cause you to turn blue and pass out, busyness without rest will cause you to *"pass out"* from things that matter. *"I am so busy."* We say this as a badge of honor, as if our exhaustion were a trophy, and our ability to withstand 70-80 hour workweeks a mark of real character. We convince ourselves that the busier we are, the more we are accomplishing and the more important we must be. But is this really so? Does more activity really mean more accomplishment? To be unavailable to friends and family, to miss the sunsets and the full moons, to blast through all our obligations without time for taking a deep breath—this has become the model of a successful life.

Can we really distinguish essentials that matter in our efforts to get more things? Just this week I worked with a very competent lady who has reached the pinnacle in her profession, with a world class apartment and a beach house for the weekends. Although her income puts her in the top 1% nationally, she has lost the sense of fulfilling work. One of her expressed goals is to *smile more on my way to happiness.*

"If you are losing your leisure, look out. You may be losing your soul."
—**Logan Pearsall Smith (1865-1946) U.S.-born British essayist, biographer, critic**

Embrace Sabbath days and times in your life. Wisdom, peace, contentment and insight about fulfilling work will grow in those times. Take a walk, give thanks for simple things, take a bath with music and candles, turn off the telephone, pager, TV and computer—carve out those times for restoration and spiritual breathing. Even Jesus got away from the crowds periodically.

FROM THE BIBLE:

"Then Jesus suggested. 'Let's get away from the crowds for a while and rest.' For so many people were coming and going that they scarcely had time to eat. So they left by boat for a quieter spot."

MARK 6:31 (TLB)

DIRECTION FOR TODAY:

How has your striving for success crowded out the Sabbath in your life?

_____

_____

_____

_____

_____

_____

_____

_____

_____

How to Lift a Toyota

When you have a clear enough "why" you will figure out the "how."

Recently I met with a couple I had seen initially eight years ago. Although they struggled with the process then, they were able to lay out some clear goals. Joyce was a nurse and she wanted to be able to stay home and possibly have a first child. They wanted to own their own home and were clear about those details. Today, their three beautiful children have a stay-at-home mommy, the family is living in the house they wanted with a paid for mortgage and Joyce and Tom are now ready to plan the next stage of their lives.

The point is this: most people stumble while trying to determine the *"what."* Before even clarifying what they want to move toward, they begin to see the obstacles: ***"I'd like a better job but I don't have a college degree." "We'd like a nicer house, but we can't afford it." "I'd love to go on a missions trip this year but my boss would never give me time off."*** A *"whatever"* vision will give you *"whatever"* results. Forget the obstacles, define a clear *"What"* and a *"Why"* and you will be amazed as the *"How"* comes into view.

> *"Reduce your plan to writing . . . the moment you do, you will add tangible form to your intangible desires, having a roadmap to success."*
> —Napoleon Hill, author best-selling classic, *Think and Grow Rich*

We have a neighbor who was severely burned in an automobile accident caused by a drunk driver. That same accident claimed the life of her daughter. She had a big "Why" and became national president of Mothers Against Drunk Drivers (MADD). What is it that you would really like to accomplish? Do you want to learn another language? Why? Do you want to go on the annual missions trip with your church? Why? If you get clear enough on the "why" you will figure out the "how."

"Every time I've made a decision just with my heart, or just with my head, it was always a bad decision. Using both is what has worked for me. To engage my heart and my head together, that's when I make the best decisions."
—Loretta Mervis, president, Wachovia's East Polk County Bank

Moral of the story: You don't need degrees, training and a seminar on how to lift a car if your child is trapped underneath one.

FROM THE BIBLE:

"The lazy man won't go outside and work. 'There might be a lion outside!' he says. He sticks to his bed like a door to its hinges! He is too tired even to lift his food from his dish to his mouth! Yet in his own opinion he is smarter than seven wise men."

PROVERBS 26: 13-16

DIRECTION FOR TODAY:

What is a goal you would like to accomplish in the next three years? Why do you want that to happen? What are you doing now to make it happen?

_____

_____

_____

_____

_____

_____

_____

Awake At Your Funeral

What will people say about you at your funeral?

Recently we attended a lavish 60th birthday party for Lynn, a counselor friend of ours. The party was given by Lynn's husband and children. Attendees were neighbors, employees, church friends, and colleagues. This was not just to honor Lynn's work, although all of us in the room have benefited from her caring, compassionate, counselor's heart. Stories told were funny, poignant, sad, and appreciative, but all reflected a life of balance, purpose and meaning.

> *"You are not here merely to make a living. You are here in order to enable the world to live more amply, with greater vision, with a finer spirit of hope and achievement. You are here to enrich the world, and you impoverish yourself if you forget the errand."*
>
> **—Woodrow Wilson**

Remember, your work is not the only evidence of a life well lived. If your work is all that gives your life meaning, you are very vulnerable. Make deposits of success in all areas of your life; in all the roles you live out. Because Lynn's work is doing something she loves, it naturally spills over into her role as a wife, mother, daughter, grandmother, sister, in-law, neighbor, friend and counselor.

During the course of the evening, Lynn commented that this was like being *"awake at your own funeral."* Hopefully, we are all living lives where we would like to be awake at our own funerals; where we would want to hear honest and unguarded comments about how our life has touched others. And it was also a reminder that we do need to express appreciation to people in our lives while they can still hear it. Choose three people this week and tell them something you would say about them at their funeral.

They say such nice things about people at their funerals that it makes me sad to realize that I'm going to miss mine by just a few days.

— Garrison Keillor

What could people say about your life—aside from what you accomplished in your work? How will you be remembered as a son or daughter? As a neighbor, church member and community participant? As a parent or spouse? What would you like to have written on your tombstone?

FROM THE BIBLE:

"And let us be concerned about one another in order to promote love and good works, not staying away from our meetings, as some habitually do, but encouraging each other, and all the more as you see the day drawing near."

HEBREWS 10: 24-25 (HCSB)

DIRECTION FOR TODAY:

Who are three people you'd like to compliment before they die? Can you do that this week?

_____

_____

_____

_____

_____

_____

_____

_____

The Hammer in the Hull

Is there a small hammer tapping out a compromising leak in your life?

Years ago a lifeboat in the London harbor sprung a leak, and while being repaired the workers found that a hammer had been left in the bottom of the hull by the builders thirteen years before. The constant motion of the boat had allowed that hammer to wear completely through the planking and to then cause a tiny hole in the plating itself.

History is full of examples of buildings falling, cars disintegrating, marriages exploding, and careers collapsing as an end result of small blunders. The majority of airplane crashes, medical malpractice cases, and business failures are caused by small compromises or deceptions.

The advent of self-service gas stations started a dramatic downhill slope in the condition of cars on our nation's roads. People began getting gas only, ignoring the inspection of belts, wiper blades and fluid levels. Then, after weeks of drowning out the brake squeak with a louder stereo system, they expressed surprise when the brakes failed completely. Those little things tend to lead to bigger problems if ignored or buried.

The dead letter department of the post office in Washington received seven million pieces of undelivered mail in one recent year. Eighty thousand of those bore no address whatever. Many were from established businesses. Are the workers responsible for those deserving of promotion? If a person is consistently ten minutes late for all-important meetings, is it any surprise that he/she is first in line for a layoff? If a husband is constantly critical of his wife's cooking, it is any wonder that she falls for the man who compliments her smallest actions?

Now is a great time to clean out your hull. Is there a small negative habit that is undermining your success? Is there a small indiscretion that is eroding a valued relationship? Make your life a Stradivarius; created with exquisite workmanship and unquestioned integrity.

For want of a nail, the shoe was lost:
For want of the shoe, the horse was lost;
For want of the horse, the rider was lost;
For want of the rider, the battle was lost;
For want of the battle, the kingdom was lost,
And all for the want of a nail.

FROM THE BIBLE:

"Well done, good and faithful servant! You have been faithful with a few things; I will put you in charge of many things. Come and share your master's happiness!"

MATTHEW 25: 21 (NIV)

DIRECTION FOR TODAY:

What is that small "hammer" that has the potential to create a hole in your life? What could you do to remove it and repair the damage?

_____

_____

_____

_____

_____

_____

_____

_____

SANCTIFIED IGNORANCE

DOES "GODLY" WORK JUSTIFY A LACK OF AUTHENTICITY?

Pastor Jones sat in my office, slouched down in the big chair, struggling to relay the events of the last few days. After 19 years of faithful service as a pastor, he had been informed that his contract would not be renewed. No matter how gentle the delivery, the message screamed out at him—he had been fired, terminated, downsized, or uninstalled. How could this happen to a man of God? A man who had committed his life to serving God in the most socially recognized path of service. The anger and sense of betrayal came exploding out as we began to explore his options for moving on.

The portrayal of the preceding years, however, relayed a series of red flags that had been ignored. Pastor Jones was now grossly overweight, having drowned some of his frustrations in eating. He was on medication for depression and was being treated for a bleeding ulcer. Were these not clear signs of a life out of balance? Doesn't God use physical unrest as a method of telling us something is out of alignment? In questioning this gentle, Godly man about his current life picture, he shared openly his naïve theological view. He simply thought that if he were committed to God, somehow everything would just work out. In his own words he said he was guilty of "sanctified ignorance." This phrase jumped out at me and has haunted me ever since.

The belief that if we love God and have committed our lives to him, everything will just work out, is an immature theology. Getting up each morning as a clean slate, just open to whatever may happen that day, will lead to a life of mediocrity. This is not the path of accomplishment, of excellence, of maximizing our impact and witness.

"The place God calls you to is the place where your deep gladness and the world's deep hunger meet."

—Fredrick Buechner

Anything you are gifted in can be used in a way that honors God—your challenge is to use your skills in ways that are true "ministry." There are gardeners who minister God's love, grace and beauty and there are preachers who scream at their children and dread going to the office. Each of us have the opportunity to find that unique path that God has called us to.

FROM THE BIBLE:

"And he has given both…the ability to teach others. He has filled them with skill to do all kinds of work as craftsmen, designers, embroiderers in blue, purple and scarlet yarn and fine linen, and weavers—all of them master craftsmen and designers. So Bezalel, Oholiab and every skilled person to whom the Lord has given skill and ability to know how to carry out all the work of constructing the sanctuary are to do the work just as the Lord has commanded."

EXODUS 35: 34—36: 1. (NIV)

DIRECTION FOR TODAY:

What unique skill do you have that can be used for God's work? Is it one that is normally thought of as a "ministry" skill?

_____

_____

_____

_____

_____

_____

_____

_____

Living My Dreams

Can we really live out our dreams or is that an "unrealistic" desire?

Recently in working with a young man, he expressed this sentiment: *"My fear is that I will discover what I love doing but by then be too old to enjoy a full life of living it out."* Wow, what an approach/avoidance conflict. Remember those from your introductory Psychology classes? You want a cookie but know that if you reach for one your hand will get slapped.

What about this above stated fear? When do you cross the line age-wise where it's just better not to want or know about a better life, but better to just exist and wait for the grave? Is it 35, 50 or 70? Is ignorance really bliss after all? I've had 27-yr-olds who are fearful that they've missed the window of opportunity for a life well lived. If your dream was to play quarterback in the Super Bowl, that may be true, but for most of us, living out our dreams is not one event.

We are hearing more and more about mid-life career changes. Early life experiences are a wonderful help in the clarification process—helping us find that one true path for the most productive season of our lives. I have had the privilege of helping a dentist become a counselor, an attorney start an Internet business, a pastor become an artist, and guiding a teacher to a fulfilling and productive season of writing.

Look for recurring themes in things that get your attention. Is it art, music, children, old people, cars, caring and nurturing, birds, reading, flying? Don't think that your dream needs to be new and revolutionary. We all know someone like Susie who sells seashells by the seashore, but most lives of fulfillment may look ordinary to an observer. We find that even those who end up extremely wealthy are not necessarily doing something rare; rather the critical element is that they are doing something they truly enjoy!

"Cherish your visions and your dreams as they are the children of your soul; the blueprints of your ultimate achievements."

— Napoleon Hill, motivational author

Your dream life will integrate your **(1) Skills & Abilities, (2) Your Personality Traits, and (3) Your Values, Dreams & Passions.** Trust your heart in this process. It's more intuition than logic. And be confident you can live out your dreams. Don't settle for less!

"You're not old until regrets take the place of dreams."

FROM THE BIBLE:

"I will pour out my Spirit on all people. Your sons and daughters will prophesy, your old men will dream dreams, your young men will see visions."

AMOS 2: 28 (NIV)

DIRECTION FOR TODAY:

What are the recurring themes of interest in your life? Have you acted on those?

_____

_____

_____

_____

_____

_____

_____

I Just Work For the Money

Ultimately money is never enough compensation for investing our time and energy.

"Law school sucked all the life and creativity out of me." "I've never been happy practicing law." "I have never had a sense of purpose." "I feel destined to do something great, but have no idea why or what." "I work only for the money."

These are statements from a young attorney—who in his last position had been sick for 6 months, *"triggered initially by stress."* But a new *"career opportunity"* presented itself and he is now working in a prestigious position with a Fortune 500 company. Unfortunately, the sickness is returning, starting with the symptoms of a choking feeling and shortness of breath.

Ultimately, money is never enough compensation for investing our time and energy. There must be a sense of meaning, purpose and accomplishment. Anything that does not blend our Values, Dreams and Passions will cause us on some level to choke. Events since 9/11/01 have caused all of us to *"reassess what's important."* A life well lived must go beyond just making a paycheck—even if it's a very large one.

The Bible tells us in Ecclesiastes 5:10; ***"Whoever loves money never has money enough; whoever loves wealth is never satisfied with his income."*** If money is the only reward of your job, you will begin to see deterioration in other areas of your life—physically, emotionally, spiritually, and relationally.

> *"That every man find pleasure in his work — this is a gift of God."*
> **—Ecclesiastes 3:13**

I have been working with a media executive—whose salary after 21 years with the same company is in excess of $330,000. In the process of taking a *"life inventory"* she says she is *"waking up to things that are important to me"* for the very first time. The intense focus on work has caused her to miss many deposits of success in other areas of her life.

Incidentally, I have to add an interesting side note here. Proper alignment in doing work we love does not mean the family will be eating rice and beans—in fact, the opposite is more often what I see occur. I have seen people increase their income by 4-5 times as they move into the freedom of finding God's authentic path for their work and lives. Proper alignment releases not only a sense of peace and accomplishment, but money is likely to break in on you like an exploding flood of fresh water.

FROM THE BIBLE:

"Has the Lord as much pleasure in your burnt offerings and sacrifices as in your obedience? Obedience is far better than sacrifice. He is much more interested in your listening to him than in your offering the fat of rams to him."

I Samuel 15: 22 (TLB)

DIRECTION FOR TODAY:

What are those dreams you have buried in the daily pressure to be "practical" and "realistic?" How could you tap into and release those for higher levels of success?

_____

_____

_____

_____

_____

_____

_____

Psychotherapy or Procrastination

Are your past "issues" really holding you back—or can you go forward in confidence today?

My academic degrees are in clinical psychology—and I believe psychotherapy is a good thing. The introspection and understanding can be very helpful in recognizing where you are today. However, I see many people use psychotherapy as a reason to postpone making helpful changes. Year after year they claim, *"I have to work through a lot of 'issues' before I can change."* Baloney! Start your changes now—How old do you have to be to draw that line in the sand and start a new day?

Are we so "sophisticated" in our understanding of man that we have to see psychotherapy as the only means for ridding us of our faults and prompting us toward positive change? And is this an attitude of recognizing the "hope that is within us" or is it a submission to weakness? Could it even be arrogance masquerading as spiritual modesty—"God's just not ready for me to move on." Can we doubt the power of God to heal us? Can we move from the psychological to the spiritual as we claim the radical possibilities of grace?

> *"People are always blaming their circumstances for what they are. I don't believe in circumstances. The people who get on in the world are the people who get up and look for the circumstances they want, and if they can't find them, make them."*
> — **George Bernard Shaw**

Don't change just because you NEED to change or because other people want you to change; change because you want more. What you are going TO is always a better long-term motivator than what you are going FROM. **Focusing on what you are going FROM tends to keep anger, resentment, bitterness, discouragement and frustration high. Getting clear on what you are going TO will release hope, optimism, boldness and enthusiasm.**

Hiding behind an inability to change is often a desire to remain the same. I do understand that the familiarity of comfortable misery may be more desirable than the unknown of potential change. But then be honest about that. If you are living the life you want to live, don't pass the responsibility onto some psychological innuendo.

If you want to change, don't get caught up in waiting to change. Remember, *"Success is the progressive realization of worthwhile goals."* You can be *"successful"* today by taking action toward your goals. Don't let me catch you hiding out on the counselor's couch because of how your mommy potty trained you. Take responsibility for who and what you are today, and start the process of becoming what you know you can be tomorrow.

FROM THE BIBLE:

"Be strong and courageous, all you who hope in the Lord."

PSALM 31: 24 (HCSB)

DIRECTION FOR TODAY:

What have you been hanging on to as an excuse for a lack of excellence? Can you claim God's resources today for the healing you need?

_____

_____

_____

_____

_____

_____

_____

_____

THE MERRY-GO-ROUND OF MY PROFES___AL LIFE

DO YOU FEEL LIKE YOUR LIFE IS MOVING FORWARD OR ARE YOU JUST GOING AROUND IN CIRCLES?

"Dan, the merry-go-round of my professional life has left me no farther than a few steps from where I got on and with a weak stomach."

Many times a career path starts because of circumstances, rather than priorities. Family expectations, chance occurrences, a friendly teacher, or seeking money can lead us down an unfulfilling career path. It's tough to make good choices at 18 that will be meaningful at 45. Just recently, I saw a 44-yr-old client who opened with the comment, "I'm tired of living my life based on the decisions made by an 18-yr-old."

"The man who does things makes mistakes, but he never makes the biggest mistake of all—doing nothing."

—Benjamin Franklin

If your work life is not providing a sense of meaning, purpose and fulfillment, draw a line in the sand. Decide what the ideal day would look like; how would you spend your time, what skills you would use. Money is ultimately never enough compensation for investing one's time and energy. There must be a sense of meaning and accomplishment. And yet a surprising thing frequently happens on the way to fulfillment and worthy contribution—rather than learning to live on "beans and rice" there is often the release of a financial flood.

A former pastor, who is now a well-known artist, relates that his income is 8-10 times what it was previously. And this while finding authenticity in his God-given uniqueness. The frustrated corporate executive who is now a web content and book writer tells me that she has reduced her work week hours by 2/3 but has increased her income 3 times over. Scott Adams, of Dilbert fame, escaped the cubicle and became a multi-millionaire with his "doodling."

"The rung of a ladder was never meant to rest upon, but only to hold a man's foot long enough to enable him to put the other somewhat higher."
                                                            —**Thomas H. Huxley**

Life is too short for "merry-go-round" sameness. If you take that image, you know that if you step off a moving merry-go-round, you will have momentum that will project you straight out in some direction. But rather than allowing that to be a random choice, think through the desired direction first. Then take that step, expecting the inertia to give you a jump start to a new level of success. Believe that a life of purpose and meaning is your best source of financial success as well. I hope it's no secret that's it's easier to make money doing something you love than doing something you hate. Success is not an accident.

FROM THE BIBLE:

"Trust in the Lord with all thine heart; and lean not unto thine own understanding. In all thy ways acknowledge him, and he shall direct thy paths."

PROVERBS 3: 5-6 (KJV)

DIRECTION FOR TODAY:

What is an area of your life where you are on a merry-go-round? How can you make that step off?

Stop That Thinking

Is staying inside the lines limiting your accomplishments and fulfillment?

Research shows that 90 percent of five-year olds are creative, but only 2 percent of adults are. Where does the decline begin? Have you been in a kindergarten classroom lately? Most are an exercise in behavior control. "Caleb, get behind Susie." "Autumn, stop pulling at your dress." "Eliza, get back over here in your chair." "Ian, stay inside the lines when you color." From the first day of school, they've been teaching you how to limit your thinking. Sit in straight rows, stay on the sidewalk, talk only when it's your turn, color inside the lines and be quiet when you eat your lunch. Is it any wonder that creativity and curiosity are drilled out of most of us at an early age?

Almost everything we are taught is modeled on repetitive, predictable tasks. *"Learn"* math, science, cooking, or construction. Just make sure you do it the *"right"* way. Our world-wide competitiveness has been compromised by the assembly line training of our educational system.

> *"Do not then train youths to learning by force and harshness, but direct them to it by what amuses their minds so that you may be better able to discover with accuracy the peculiar bent of the genius of each."*
>
> **—Plato**

At every circus, we see the elephants. Usually, there is a rope attaching one of their legs to a small stake. How is it that a small stake in the ground can control a huge animal? When they are still babies, they're tied to a thick tree with a heavy chain. Over time, the chain is replaced with a lighter one, and the tree is replaced with a stake in the ground. The behavior control has become its own self-inflicted prison. Now, we aren't little elephants, but studies abound that show how those early experiences can create ruts and limiting expectations that control us the rest of our lives.

"What lies behind us and what lies before us are tiny matters compared to what lies within us."

—**Oliver Wendell Holmes**

In today's work environment, if we are not able to think, we will quickly lose our place of productivity. Repetitive tasks can be duplicated by robots and machinery. Commit to being a *"knowledge worker"* and a *"continuous learner."* No matter what your age, foster your own passionate curiosity, imagination, creativity and love of learning. As you release your natural creativity, life will again become more meaningful, satisfying and enjoyable.

FROM THE BIBLE:

"Train a child in the way he should go (is bent), and when he is old he will not turn from it."

PROVERBS 22:6 (NIV)

DIRECTION FOR TODAY:

How could creative thinking improve something in your work life today?

_____

_____

_____

_____

_____

_____

_____

ENGAGE THE IMAGINATION AND THE BODY W FOLLOW

IF THINKING PRECEDES REALITY, WHERE IS YOUR THINKING LEADING YOU?

Advertising wizard Roy Williams once said, *"Engage the imagination, then take it where you will. Where the mind has repeatedly journeyed, the body will surely follow. People go only to places they have already been in their minds."*

> **"Imagination rules the world."**   **—Napoleon**

Wow—thus the power behind spending 2.3 million dollars for a 30-second Super Bowl ad. Marketing people believe that if they can get us to imagine something, our actions and pocketbooks will follow.

This principle can greatly enhance your life or destroy you. An affair of infidelity never takes place instantly; rather it is the fulfillment of where the mind has already been many times. Physical vitality or sports excellence comes only after *"seeing"* it happen in advance. Financial success or ruin follows being able to *"imagine"* it well before the actual arrival.

> **"Most of my ideas belonged to other people who didn't bother to develop them."**
> **—Thomas Edison**

Career or business success follows being able to see it in advance. What do you *"see"* in your future? Do you see failure?—then it will surely follow. Do you see success?—then nothing can stop you. Need a job? Do you *"see"* that companies are laying off and no one is hiring—or do you *"see"* like the young man who got 6 job offers in

10 days—in a specialized chemical research field—with no experience and a very recent college degree?

Want to start your own business? Do you *"imagine"* that 4 out of 5 new businesses fail or could you *"see"* helping single mothers find shared housing and in the process create a $144,000 income like Carmel Sullivan did? http://www.co-abode.com

Sounds surprisingly like the Biblical adage, **"As a man thinketh in his heart, so is he."** Ps. 23:7 Guard your thinking; let it lead your body and actions to positive results.

"He who cherishes a beautiful vision, a lofty ideal in his heart, will one day realize it. Dream lofty dreams and as you dream so shall you become..."
— **James Allen**

FROM THE BIBLE:

"Thank you for making me so wonderfully complex! It is amazing to think about. Your workmanship is marvelous—and how well I know it."

PSALM 139: 14 (TLB)

DIRECTION FOR TODAY:

Is your imagination engaged today? What is the picture it is creating for you?

_____

_____

_____

_____

_____

_____

_____

THE SHALLOW WATERS OF AVARICE

IS THE PURSUIT OF MONEY TAKING YOU AWAY FROM YOUR REAL HEART'S DESIRE AND CALLING?

The lead-in question on the information requested when I work with someone personally is this: *"Briefly describe your current work situation."* Here is a recent response: *"Antithetical to my personal and professional expectations. Unfulfilling on multiple levels: Lack of meaning and purpose; a myopic pursuit of the almighty dollar; a parasitic and never ending voyage into the shallow waters of avarice."* Wow—what a powerful and eloquent statement of being off track. And of the understanding that money is never enough compensation for investing one's time and energy.

This young man continued: *"Because of the necessity and immediacy of my situation . . . I took the path of least resistance which has led me down a perilous pike of disappointment and despair. As a direct result of our financial obligations, I absolved myself of the freedom to easily pursue my dreams for the oppressive restraints of debt."* Feeling trapped by the realities of life, he felt blocked from any attempts at following his true passions.

Fortunately, new possibilities are possible. I helped this young man map out a process for getting an additional degree and an immediate plan for expression of his unique writing skills. He can hike, run a marathon, study fossils with his kids and get involved in a book club. Life does not have to be put on hold. There are always ways to make deposits of success in areas deemed important. There are few obstacles beyond those existing in our minds, if we are creative in looking for solutions. And remember to enjoy the journey, starting with today. Success is not a future event—it is the *"progressive realization of worthwhile goals."* Thus, either you are successful today or you are not.

Money never made a man happy yet, nor will it. There is nothing in its nature to produce happiness. The more a man has, the more he wants. Instead of its filling a vacuum, it makes one. If it satisfies one want, it doubles and trebles that

want another way. That was a true proverb of the wise man, rely upon it; "Better is little with the fear of the Lord, than great treasure, and trouble therewith."
—**Benjamin Franklin (1706 - 1790)**

Look for opportunities to rise above the *"shallow waters of avarice."* Do something noble today!

FROM THE BIBLE:

"For the love of money is the first step toward all kinds of sin. Some people have even turned away from God because of their love for it, and as a result have pierced themselves with many sorrows."

I TIMOTHY 6: 10 (TLB)

DIRECTION FOR TODAY:

How could you better engage your passions AND provide for your financial needs?

_____

_____

_____

_____

_____

_____

_____

_____

_____

IS THERE STILL TIME FOR ME TO
MAKE M⋯E COUNT

IS THERE A TIME OR AGE WHEN OUR LIVES BECOME UNPRODUCTIVE?

Recently I saw a 27-yr-old as a coaching client who asked the question at the top of this page. And then he continued; *"Tell me that just because I started in (his profession) . . . doesn't mean my life will be filed away. . . . Encourage me to find a 'motivating desire' once more. I think I've lost it."*

What do you think? Is it too late for this misdirected 27-yr-old? When do we reach the point of no return and have to settle for the life we have chosen or had chosen for us?

Thomas Edison's teachers said he was *"too stupid to learn anything."* He was fired from his first two jobs for being *"non-productive."* As an inventor, Edison made 10,000 unsuccessful attempts at inventing the light bulb. When a reporter asked, *"How did it feel to fail 10,000 times?"* Edison replied, *"I didn't fail 10,000 times. The light bulb was an invention with 10,000 steps."*

Walt Disney was fired by a newspaper editor because *"he lacked imagination and had no good ideas."* He went bankrupt several times before he built Disneyland. In fact, the proposed park was rejected by the city of Anaheim on the grounds that it would only attract riffraff.

Bill Gates, Michael Dell, Maya Angelou and Michelle Pfieffer are all college dropouts. Did they forfeit their opportunities for success when they *"dropped out?"*

Often people attempt to live their lives backwards: they try to have more things, or more money, in order to do more of what they want so that they will be happier.

The way it actually works is the reverse. You must first be who you really are, then, do what you need to do, in order to have what you want.

—Margaret Young

Life experience is a wonderful teacher and clarifier. The process of finding God's will and purpose for our lives is not easily done at 18, 22 or 27 years of age. Welcome the unfolding process of understanding your talents, dreams and passions. Enjoy the journey of discovery, recognizing that even the unpleasant experiences are useful tools for providing more clarity. Many of the people I work with are in their 40s and 50s. My belief is that if you are able at 45 to discover your *"mission,"* you can then begin to enjoy the most productive and fulfilling 20 years of your life. At every stage, look for varied life experiences, make deposits of success physically, spiritually, in personal development, and in relationships, and enjoy the wonderful process of *"life."*

FROM THE BIBLE:

"This is the day the Lord has made; let us rejoice and be glad in it."

PSALM 118: 24 (NIV)

DIRECTION FOR TODAY:

Have you reached your peak, or are you moving into the most successful season of your life?

We All Need Somebody To Lean On

It's important to find people who encourage and help us "see" our greatest possibilities.

One of our primary needs as human beings is to feel the support of those around us. Ideally, that will mean we are nurtured and encouraged by our nuclear family first and then by an ever-widening circle of relatives, friends, teachers, etc. Without that support, we tend to be less and less willing to try new things or to go down non-traditional paths. Too frequently the gifted artist does not hear, *"I really think you can do it"* but rather, *"You know artists don't make any money"* or something to that effect. The guy with a critical wife stays in a job where he is *"underemployed"* because he doesn't feel the freedom to stretch his wings. An employee who is punished for making a mistake will ultimately do the very least to maintain her job, not willing to risk the disapproval again. A pastor who is constantly criticized will retreat into eating or TV watching rather than focusing on the great potential of the church.

Not having someone to lean on, adding other's fear to his own, the next Bill Gates or Thomas Edison settles into the twilight world of could-have-beens and regrets. Without encouragement during the many falls, a baby would never learn to walk. Most businesspeople *"fail"* 3-4 times before they ultimately find the right business and methods for their success.

I fear that the current environment of isolation, where we no longer have sidewalks and community churches, but rather cubicles and remote opened garage doors, has crippled the creativity of this generation. Without the sounding board of and encouragement from those around us we will gravitate toward very minimal accomplishment. Lack of support leads to minimal effectiveness. That's why one of the most important characteristics of very successful people is that they spend time with people who are performing at the level at which they want to perform. Find those people in your own life and watch your success soar.

No wonder the ongoing popularity of the 1972 song, *"Lean on Me."* Here's the chorus:

Lean on me, when you're not strong And I'll be your friend, I'll help you carry on For, it won't be long Til I'm gonna need somebody to lean on*

*For complete lyrics: **http://tinyurl.com/29hql***

FROM THE BIBLE:

"Two are better than one, because they have a good return for their work: If one falls down, his friend can help him up. But pity the man who falls and has no one to help him up!

ECCLESIASTES 4: 10 (NIV)

DIRECTION FOR TODAY:

Who are the 2-3 people in your life you can "lean" on? How have they helped you to become more than you would have on your own?

_____

_____

_____

_____

_____

_____

_____

_____

The Peter Principle

Getting "promoted" could move you away from what you do well.

The popular little book titled *"The Peter Principle"* was written in 1969. After studying hundreds of organizations, the author, Laurence Peter, concluded that *"in a hierarchy every employee tends to rise to his/her level of incompetence."* We've all seen it happen: the great bank teller who gets moved up to branch manager only to leave in disgrace for not being able to sell new business or to manage employees. The sales rep that gets promoted to territory manager but cannot discipline his former buddies. The best construction worker who is asked to be project overseer but leaves in anger because he could not understand the budget forecasts.

The author thus proposed that the best *"work is accomplished by those employees who have not yet reached their level of incompetence."* But isn't this just a matter of learning new skills and growing in responsibilities? Perhaps—but frequently it is simply taking someone out of what he/she does well and putting them into an area that does not match their strongest abilities at all.

> *"Comrades, you have lost a good captain to make him an ill general."*
> —**Michel de Montaigne (1533–1592)**

One of the keys to living out our calling is to be doing work that blends our *(1) Skills & Abilities, (2) Personality Traits,* and *(3) our Values, Dreams & Passions.* Think how frequently we see this violated when someone is *"promoted:"* The quiet introvert who is thrust into the middle of office interaction; the analytical person who is forced to represent the company in a sales and marketing role. The best nursery teacher in the school is not necessarily the best candidate for school principal. A great youth pastor may be miserable as a senior pastor. This isn't a matter of unwillingness—

we have to realize that even *"open doors"* and *"opportunities"* can lead us away from God's ideal path. The key is to know ourselves and see confirmation of God's preparation in other ways as well.

In today's volatile workplace people are often forced to move from organization to organization. In many ways, this is a positive occurrence. Rather than being expected to move vertically up the ranks to a position of incompetence, you can address your strongest areas of competence and again apply them in a new organization or opportunity.

FROM THE BIBLE:

"God has given each of you some special abilities; be sure to use them to help each other, passing on to others God's many kinds of blessings. Are you called to preach? Then preach as though God himself were speaking through you. Are you called to help others? Do it with all the strength and energy that God supplies, so that God will be glorified through Jesus Christ.."

I Peter 4: 10-11 (TLB)

DIRECTION FOR TODAY:

Do you know your strongest "areas of competence?" Are you using those effectively each day?

_____

_____

_____

_____

_____

_____

_____

CRUSHED SPIRIT

HOW CAN WE COMBAT THE INEVITABLE CIRCUMSTANCES OF LIFE AND MAINTAIN A POSITIVE SPIRIT?

A 61-yr-old gentleman who lost his job seven months earlier came to see me for Life Coaching.. When a long period of time has passed without a job I always suspect more life issues to be lurking in the sidelines. Yes, his wife left him four months ago, his daughter *("the joy of my life")* got married and moved away five months ago, his investments were now worth less than half what they were 3 years ago, he had worked for the same company for 36 years and now they let him go with a small severance package, he's unconnected at his church and feels *"rejected on all sides."* He made the last mortgage payment three weeks ago on his dream house that now must be sold to settle the divorce and he'll likely move into an apartment in town.

Where do we go from here? Proverbs 18:14 tells us *"A man's spirit sustains him in sickness, but a crushed spirit who can bear?"* Or in The Living Bible *"what hope is left?"*

> *"Times of general calamity and confusion create great minds.*
> *   The purest ore is produced from the hottest furnace, and the brightest thunderbolt is elicited from the darkest storms."*
> **— Charles Caleb Colton (1780–1832)**

Each area of our lives requires that we are making deposits of success. Tiny withdrawals with no deposits will lead to bankruptcy in relationships, physically, spiritually, and socially as well as in jobs and finances. I know that in crisis the area of most pain gets most of our attention. But often it is by making extra deposits in other areas that a person can springboard back to success in even the most critical ones.

My advice: Set aside time for vigorous physical exercise. Walk 3 miles—the feeling will help cleanse and stimulate creativity. Seek out a Godly mentor. Much of the success of AA has been in having another person to call in the lowest times. Read the Bible and other inspirational material at least 2 hours daily. Volunteer for a worthy cause. Helping someone else in need is a great way to ease the inward pain. Get a job—even if it's not your dream job or a great career move. Deliver pizzas or work in the garden department at Home Depot—to get moving in a positive direction while you continue to build for long term success.

"People are like stained-glass windows. They sparkle and shine when the sun is out, but when the darkness sets in, their true beauty is revealed only if there is a light from within."

— **Elizabeth Kübler-Ross**

Unfortunately, some losses are irretrievable and some pain is debilitating. If you recognize too many withdrawals in your life, take drastic measures to stop the hemorrhaging—today!

FROM THE BIBLE:

"A joyful heart makes a face cheerful, but a sad heart produces a broken spirit."

PROVERBS 15: 13 (HCSB)

DIRECTION FOR TODAY:

What are you doing to keep your spirit strong today?

_____

_____

_____

_____

_____

_____

THE KING'S FOUR WIVES

DON'T IGNORE YOUR "WIVES." THEY MAY TAKE CARE OF YOU IN COMING YEARS.

Once upon a time there was a rich king who had four wives. He loved his fourth wife the most and adorned her with riches. He also loved his third wife and was always showing her off to neighboring kingdoms. However, he always feared that she would leave him. His second wife was kind and considerate and his trusted confidante and advisor in difficult times. Wife number one was devoted and loyal and although she loved him deeply, he was not so interested and tended to ignore her.

One day, the king fell ill and knew his time was short. He thought of his luxurious life and feared being alone when he died.

He asked his fourth wife, *"I have loved you the most, endowed you with the finest clothing and showered great care over you. Now that I'm dying, will you follow me and keep me company?"* *"No way!"* she replied and walked away without another word.

The sad king then asked the third wife, *"I have loved you all my life. Now that I'm dying, will you follow me and keep me company?"* *"No!"* she replied. *"Life is too good! When you die, I'm going to remarry!"*

He then asked the second wife, *"I have always turned to you for help and you've always been there for me. When I die, will you follow me and keep me company?"* *"I'm sorry, I can't help you out this time!"* she replied. *"At the very most, I can help with your funeral."*

Then a voice called out to the king in his sadness: *"I'll leave with you and follow you no matter where you go."* The king looked up and there was his first wife. She was so skinny and undernourished. Greatly grieved, the king said, *"I should have taken much better care of you when I had the chance!"*

In truth, we all have four wives in our lives. Our fourth wife is our body. No matter how much time and effort we lavish in making it look good, it'll leave us when we die. Our third wife is our possessions, status and wealth. When we die, it will all go to others. Our second wife is our family and friends. No matter how much they have been there for us, the closest they can stay by us is up to the grave. And our first wife is our soul, often neglected in pursuit of wealth, power and pleasures of the ego. However, our soul is the only thing that will follow us wherever we go.

The moral: Look after your body and keep it healthy so you can live life to its fullest. Enjoy your possessions and the comfort they provide. Cherish your friends and family and the love they provide. But don't forget to nourish your soul—it is the source of all your life and your most faithful friend. —*Source Unknown*

FROM THE BIBLE:

"Beloved, I wish above all things that thou mayest prosper and be in health, even as thy soul prospereth."

III JOHN 2 (KJV)

DIRECTION FOR TODAY:

How can you show more respect for and take care of your four wives today?

_____

_____

_____

_____

_____

_____

_____

_____

Jelly On My Hands

Yes, some people just delight in pointing out our weaknesses.

The comic strip, *Peanuts*, has some excellent examples of the obstacles we all encounter. One of my favorite examples involves Lucy and her little brother, Linus, who is constantly hanging onto his security blanket.

In this particular cartoon, Linus is in the kitchen, eating a jelly sandwich. As he finishes the sandwich, for the first time in his life, he notices the hand that held the sandwich. He begins to admire the hand. Then, without realizing it, he drops his security blanket and admires the other hand. He begins to imagine that with these hands he could be anything: the CEO of a company, a great leader, a pro basketball player, a surgeon, a novelist—even the President!

Excited about his discovery and the potential his hands hold, he runs into the next room where Lucy is watching television and shouts, *"Lucy! Lucy! Look at my hands!"*

Lucy looks at his hands, then looks into his eyes and says, *"They've got jelly on them."*

"Treat every person with kindness and respect, even those who are rude to you. Remember that you show compassion to others not because of who they are but because of who you are."

—**Andrew T. Somers**

Now you may have people around you who seem to point out the jelly on your hands rather than seeing your real potential. Don't be guilty of living up to other's low expectations. I see people every day who have given up on their sunny dreams of fulfillment and success, settling into the twilight world of could-have-beens and regrets. What do you want the next 5 years to hold for you?

"Opposition is a natural part of life. Just as we develop our physical muscles through overcoming opposition - such as lifting weights—we develop our character muscles by overcoming challenges and adversity."

—**Stephen Covey**

Need help getting past the "jelly" in your life? Take a fresh look at your unique skills and abilities, your personality assets, and your values, dreams and passions. From those you can define your path toward extraordinary greatness.

For more steps toward a Life Plan:
http://www.48days.com/

FROM THE BIBLE:

"Don't criticize, and then you won't be criticized. For others will treat you as you treat them."

MATTHEW 7: 1-2 (TLB)

DIRECTION FOR TODAY:

What can you do today to rise above the people who are pointing out the "jelly" on your hands?

_____

_____

_____

_____

_____

_____

_____

I Just Want Security, Great Pay and No Stress

Can we really expect success to be guaranteed in advance of creating results?

I had a young man come in as a client who wants to find a *"stable, secure and enjoyable"* career path. He received a degree in marketing six years ago but has been frustrated in the jobs he has had. Employers seem to want clear results from his efforts and he resists being pushed so hard. He clearly stated that he wants a job with security, no stress, and at least $45K that he will find enjoyable.

Unfortunately, he has the process reversed. He is standing in front of the stove of life saying, *"Give me heat and then I'll put some wood in."* Life does not respond to that message with anything but disappointment. Security, great pay and no stress are the result of doing something you love—and doing it with excellence. They are not something we can approach directly. They are by products of living out your values and vision. Looking for a job that pays well is addressing the circumstance and is likely to be a band-aid solution to your unrest. Clear purpose and meaning lead to greater self-esteem, confidence, boldness, enthusiasm, security, contentment, and ultimately money. Lack of opportunity is often nothing more than lack of purpose or direction.

> *"The man who does not work for the love of work but only for money is not likely to make money nor to find much fun in life."*
>
> **—Charles M. Schwab**

In the classic book, *Think and Grow Rich*, Napoleon Hill defines the process he discovered for finding fulfilling work. One of the steps is *"offer to go to work on probation."* What a radical idea; to go to work on a trial basis to see if your efforts are convincing. What a different approach to today's young job-seeker who often looks for guaranteed pay, benefits, and security in advance.

Mr. Hill says, *"The difference in income, in advancement, and in gaining recognition will save years of hard work at small pay. It has many advantages, the main one being that it will often save from one to five years of time in reaching a chosen goal."*

The biggest mistake you can make is to believe you work for someone else.

—Unknown

In a day when job searches can stretch to 12-14 months, what are the chances someone would provide an opportunity based on guaranteed results?? If someone approached you and said let me work for free for 30 days and then we'll determine what I'm worth, would you allow him/her to do so?

"Opportunity dances with those who are already on the dance floor."

— H. Jackson Brown Jr.

FROM THE BIBLE:

"Work hard so God can say to you, 'Well done.' Be a good workman, one who does not need to be ashamed when God examines your work. Know what his Word says and means."

II TIMOTHY 2: 15 (TLB)

DIRECTION FOR TODAY:

What actions can you take today to move into an arena of fulfillment—even if there is no guarantee in advance?

_____

_____

_____

_____

_____

So How's That Working For You

Self-defeating actions will continue to give us self-defeating results.

I love to hear David Letterman give his *Words of Wisdom* from Dr. Phil. The clips are absolutely hilarious. While the segments are funny when taken out of context, Dr Phil has made a national reputation for himself in providing no-nonsense advice on a variety of topics. And I have found his books to be surprisingly solid and full of direct, take-responsibility principles.

Three years ago I met with Bill, a frustrated on-the-road salesman. He knew he was off track and we laid out a plan for his exit and redirection to a more suitable and ful-filling career path. Two weeks ago Bill came in to see me again. He is still working in the same job, is even more frustrated and is now experiencing shortness of breath and chest pains. Dr. Phil's standard question comes to me often in these situations: *"So, how's that working for you?"*

Why do we continue to do what is frustrating and unfulfilling? Once we know our gifts, we have the responsibility to exercise those gifts for our own betterment and for the lives of those around us. I believe we have not only the opportunity but the accountability to live lives of fulfillment and accomplishment. I fear standing in front of God on the Day of Judgment having squandered my talents and abilities.

> *"I do not understand my own actions. For I do not do what I want, but I do the very thing I hate."*
> —**St. Paul**

The modern definition of "insanity" is to continue doing what we've always done, and yet to expect different results. But no, different results always require different actions.

I always wonder what a person has been thinking in the time between clearly understanding self-defeating behavior and the time when they decide to take action to correct it. Why would anyone continue to go to a job where they are belittled, under-paid and dishonored? Why would someone continue to do something physically that was shown to be destroying their health? Why would a husband continue to criticize and condemn his wife and then watch her recoil and cringe at his approach? Why don't we all move directly toward healthier relationships, fulfilling work and meaningful relationships, once we know the path? Why would any of us purposely choose misery over the possibility of joy and victory?

In defending the sameness of negative actions I can hear Dr. Phil's question resonating: *"So, how's that working for you?"*

FROM THE BIBLE:

"As a dog returns to its vomit, so a fool repeats his foolishness."

PROVERBS 26: 11

DIRECTION FOR TODAY:

How can you choose life, health, and love in your actions today?

_____

_____

_____

_____

_____

_____

_____

_____

_____

First Your Thinking — Then Your Life

Are you letting inaccurate information determine the quality of your day?

Ihad a lot of fun with creative experiments while getting my graduate degrees in Psychology. Students are known for devising interesting experiments to test various human theories. A number of years ago, some students decided to use one of their friends as a guinea pig, to see if false suggestions could cause reactions in the body. On the chosen day, the guinea pig left the dorm, suspecting nothing unusual. However, a friend greeted him with, *"Good Morning, Chuck! How are you doing today? You look a little pale."* Seconds later another friend rounded the corner with *"Chuck, are you feeling okay? You look a little sick!"* A third friend greeted Chuck and said, *"You really shouldn't be out of bed! You look horrible!"* Before the young man could get to his first class, he turned around, went back to the dormitory and fell into bed. He was in fact, sick.

> *"The greater part of our happiness or misery depends on our dispositions, and not on our circumstances."*
>
> **—Martha Washington**

Has anyone been feeding you false information lately? Maybe the newspapers are in on a big joke—telling you no one is hiring. Your *"friends"* have been misinformed—you really are competent and capable. Your boss is a bozo, not you. What would happen if rather than listening to the feedback, you decided to *"see"* and create your own future? Isn't there just as much likelihood that you could create a good, clean, positive future?

> *"As a man thinketh in his heart, so is he."*   **—Proverbs 23:7**

There is a lot of evidence that we can lead our thinking with our actions. In teaching Introductory Psychology I would challenge the students. Many would come to that first morning class with their heads down, shoulders drooping and a frown on their face. It was obvious the kind of day they were anticipating. I would present the challenge to jump out of bed, walk with a spring in their step, pull those shoulders back, head up with a smile—and see if by 10:00 AM they did not expect a great day.

> *"Keep your face to the sunshine and you cannot see the shadow. It's what sunflowers do."*
> — **Helen Keller**

> *"Think you can or think you can't; either way you're right."*   —**Henry Ford**

FROM THE BIBLE:

"Praise the Lord, O my soul; all my inmost being, praise his holy name. Praise the Lord, O my soul, and forget not all his benefits—who forgives all your sins and heals all your diseases, who redeems your life from the pit and crowns you with love and compassion, who satisfies your desires with good things so that your youth is renewed like the eagle's."

PSALM 103: 1-5 (NIV)

DIRECTION FOR TODAY:

What messages have you been listening to that may in fact be inaccurate?

_____

_____

_____

_____

_____

_____

A "Simple" Man

In Proverbs 7:7 we read, *"I saw among the simple, I noticed among the young men, a youth who lacked judgment."* Another translation says, *"void of understanding."* I have read this hundreds of times and have always assumed that *"simple"* actually meant a guy who just wasn't too bright—maybe a little slow—you know, one wheel in the sand. However, my new study Bible has a note: *"The person who has no purpose in life is simple-minded. Without aim or direction, an empty life is unstable, vulnerable to many temptations."* (Life Application Study Bible)

Wow—all of a sudden I see that very differently. *"No purpose, no direction."* This is not a function of IQ or education. This can be true of a Rhodes scholar or the valedictorian of your graduating class. And what happens to a person with no purpose? He/she is vulnerable to whatever circumstances come along. Get a job offer working in the salt mine—sure, why not. It's a job. Chance to go back to law school, of course. Cousin Vinny was a mobster, why don't you be one too. Okay!

Zig Ziglar talks about being a "wandering generality." Athletes don't win races, CEOs don't gain positions, ladies aren't great mothers, and scientists don't create new formulas without having specific goals defined in advance. Having a specific plan is like harnessing the power of Niagara Falls to create a massive amount of electricity.

> *"Give me a stock clerk with a goal and I will give you a man who will make history. Give me a man without a goal, and I will give you a stock clerk."*
> — **J.C. Penney**

Don't be a 45-yr-old college educated *"simple"* person. Finding your purpose and calling are critical and must precede any reasonable life choices. Clear goals in each area of your life keeps you focused on the positive goal.

Incidentally, the *"simple"* young man in the Proverbs verse goes on to spend the night with a very disreputable lady. He *"followed her like an ox going to the slaughter, like a deer stepping into a noose."* Don't let unclear direction open you to a similarly disastrous fate!

FROM THE BIBLE:

"For the Lord grants wisdom! His every word is a treasure of knowledge and understanding. He grants good sense to the godly—his saints. He is their shield, protecting them and guarding their pathway. He shows how to distinguish right from wrong, how to find the right decision every time. For wisdom and truth will enter the very center of your being, filling your life with joy."

PROVERBS 2: 6-10 (TLB)

DIRECTION FOR TODAY:

What are you doing today that proves you are not "among the simple?"

_____

_____

_____

_____

_____

_____

_____

_____

_____

_____

MEANWHILE MY MERCEDES MASKS MY MISERY

How's that for some tongue twisting alliteration? While working with a high-level professional he said this: *"Dan, I'm trying to compensate myself for what I have to go through every day. I'm trying to buy happiness because I hate my job so much."*

Now think a minute about what the counterpart of those comments may be. With work you love, a much simpler lifestyle may be very enjoyable. That may be why the typical millionaire wears inexpensive suits and drives a three year old automobile. Half of them have lived in the same home for more than twenty years. One in ten has never paid more than $47 for a watch. (According to ***The Millionaire Next Door***—by Thomas Stanley)

The really brilliant millionaires are those who selected work that they love—frequently one that has few competitors but generates high profits. They tell us ***"If you love, absolutely love what you are doing, chances are excellent that you will succeed."***

So the call of the "successful" life is a call to **authenticity**—not necessarily to poverty or to riches, but to the expression of those gifts and talents that God has uniquely given to each of us. We must seek work that provides a sense of fulfillment, accomplishment and meaning independently of the money generated. Our work must blend our (1) Skills & Abilities, (2) Personality Traits, and (3) Values, Dreams & Passions. Having the **ability** to do something well is not enough reason to invest your time and energy there. The professional referenced above had proven his ***ability*** to do the work he was expected to perform. His patients respected him and kept him very busy in his practice.

> *"We have too many people who live without working, and we have altogether too many who work without living."* —**Dean Charles R. Brown**

In the case of the mentioned professional, we have created a new business plan. One that removes him totally from patient contact yet builds on his professional training and experience. He has formed a buying cooperative for his professional group and is enlisting members aggressively. His daily time commitments are reduced dramatically, yet early projections show that his income will increase dramatically—not decrease. This is the commonly surprising result of finding an authentic application of one's talents and dreams.

Incidentally, I just bought a gorgeous new watch. My old one needed a new battery—but I mentioned to Joanne that I just wanted to look for a new watch. I found one in an outlet store in Pigeon Forge, TN while visiting the area. The box said $199.95 but I bought it for $9.95. Now if I could just take a tiny pen and write Rolex on it I could impress you even more.

FROM THE BIBLE:

"You have made known to me the path of life; you will fill me with joy in your presence, with eternal pleasures at your right hand."

PSALM 16:11 (NIV)

DIRECTION FOR TODAY:

Are you enjoying an authentic, simple life, or are you trying to buy happiness?

STOP PRAYING

SOMETIMES PRAYING BECOMES AN EXCUSE FOR INDECISION OR LACK OF ACTION.

Yes, I'm sure I'm already getting heat from some of you for this lead-in. Certainly, praying is always the preferred response. No, it's not. In my continuing rampage about lack of action, I am now maintaining that sometimes praying is not in your best interest—action is.

And I'm not just pulling this out of a hat. In the Bible book of Exodus we see the story of Moses leading those whining, complaining people through the desert. After the miraculous exit from Egypt and escape from their captors, the people are now convinced the Egyptian army is coming to get them. And they are sitting on their backsides, wringing their hands about how awful things are. Life just isn't fair.

And what did God tell them to do? In verse 15 of chapter 14, we read, ***"Then the Lord said to Moses, 'Quit praying and get the people moving! Forward, march!'"*** (The Living Bible)

Oh yes, some of you Biblical scholars will be quick to remind me of the often used verse in Isaiah 40: 31. *"But they that wait upon the Lord shall renew their strength; they shall mount up with wings as eagles; they shall run, and not be weary; and they shall walk, and not faint."* Doesn't that give encouragement to just *"wait?"* Unfortunately for slackers, that word *"wait"* comes from the same word from which we get *"waiter"* and the real meaning implies to be active doing what we know needs to be done.

> *"It is good to dream, but it is better to dream and work. Faith is mighty, but action with faith is mightier. Desiring is helpful, but work and desire are invincible."*
> **—Thomas Robert Gaines**

I get rather impatient with some people when the mortgage is due, the children are hungry and the lights are about to be cut off and they are still just praying about what to do. I know what to do; quit hiding behind your pious excuse for inactivity—and start moving.

"Indecision and delays are the parents of failure."
—George Canning, English statesman

Oh and yes, God did "save" the people that day—based on their getting up and moving forward. Once they got the idea they were participants in their success, I'll bet they ran rather than walked.

FROM THE BIBLE:

"But Moses told the people, 'Don't be afraid. Just stand where you are and watch, and you will see the wonderful way the Lord will rescue you today. The Egyptians you are looking at—you will never see them again. The Lord will fight for you, and you won't need to lift a finger!' Then the Lord said to Moses, 'Quit praying and get the people moving! Forward, march!

Exodus 14: 13-15 (TLB)

DIRECTION FOR TODAY:

What is an area in your life where you really know what to do but have been justifying "waiting?"

_____

_____

_____

_____

_____

_____

My Boss is Satan's Offspring

It's really not difficult to determine a person's point of reference.

No, I really didn't make that up. As usual, the rich life stories I hear in working with people in transition offer enough real anecdotes that I don't have to be very creative in finding phrases that colorfully describe real situations.

In anticipation of meeting with me, a very *"successful"* young lady wrote this in her pre-coaching form: *"My company is going in a strictly money-motivated direction, and my manager may very well be Satan's offspring."* She further validated her suspicions with lots of examples that certainly convinced me she might be accurate. While we saw the humor in her portrayal I also helped her go through a list to confirm the possibility of a less than Godly work environment.

> Here's the checklist to tell if your boss is Satan's offspring:
> No Morality Left
> Hatred and fighting
> Jealously and anger
> Constant effort to get the best for only himself
> Complaints and criticisms
> The feeling that everyone else is wrong except those in his own little group
> Envy, drunkenness, wild parties

This list is actually a mixture of this lady's stories and another source I refer to frequently. If it sounds a little familiar, you might want to check the list yourself in Galatians 5:19-23 (The Living Bible).

"Keep away from angry, short-tempered men, lest you learn to be like them and endanger your soul."
—**Proverbs 22: 24-25**

It's a well-known fact that we tend to take on the characteristics of those around us. We recognize this phenomenon easily in children. Clothing, music, foods and slang expressions all quickly become a reflection of the group of friends involved. We do much the same as adults.

Fortunately, we also have a list of what to expect with a Godly boss:

Love, joy, peace, patience, kindness, goodness, faithfulness, gentleness and self-control. Not too difficult to tell your boss's allegiance, is it?

FROM THE BIBLE:

"But when the Holy Spirit controls our lives he will produce this kind of fruit in us: love, joy, peace, patience, kindness, goodness, faithfulness, gentleness and self-control..."

GALATIANS 5: 22-23 (TLB)

DIRECTION FOR TODAY:

What kind of influences are you putting yourself into today? Can you choose more positive ones?

_____

_____

_____

_____

_____

_____

_____

_____

THE ROOT OF ALL EVIL

HOW SHOULD WE UNDERSTAND THIS BASIC BIBLICAL PRINCIPLE?

Well, we know the root of all evil is money, right? No, of course not; this is not the Biblical principle at all. It's the *love* of money that is the root of all evil. Now, who do you see loving money more; a rich person or a poor person?

I don't hear the wealthy people I know talking about money incessantly like I hear poor people, who seem to relate everything they do to the issue of how much money it will cost or generate. And who really is slave to money; the person who is doing something they love and in the process making $250,000 a year? No, it's the person who is going to a job he/she hates every day, JUST FOR THE MONEY—Now there's a person who has made money their god. There's the person who focuses on and loves money.

We have some dear friends who have hearts of gold—they are some of the most generous people I know. They have supported multiple worthy causes over the years, have given away cars, furniture, food and clothing to those in need and yet continue to have money come to them in massive amounts. The sale of one recent investment just added another $32 million to their resources. I never hear them talk about money—they live a modest lifestyle and are simply faithful stewards of God's riches.

> *"If you are going to let the fear of poverty govern your life . . . your reward will be that you will eat, but you will not live."* —**George Bernard Shaw**

This is a difficult point for most people. A lot of us retain something of the old primitive religious idea that poverty and self-sacrifice are pleasing to God. Somehow this implies that God has finished his work, has made all that he can make, and so the majority of people must stay poor because there's not enough to go around. So they're embarrassed to ask for much as it may deprive someone else of having their needs met.

But obviously, the reverse is true. The best way to help the poor is to not be one of them.

The desire for riches is simply the innate capacity for growth and fulfillment. In 1910, Wallace Wattles wrote, *"That which makes you want more money is the same as that which makes the plant grow; it is life seeking fuller expression."* What God requires is that we use our talents wisely—and in doing so, what I typically see is a release of peace, sense of accomplishment, and MONEY.

FROM THE BIBLE:

"Woe to you, scribes and Pharisees, hypocrites! You pay a tenth of mint, dill, and cumin, yet you have neglected the more important matters of the law—justice, mercy, and faith. These things should have been done without neglecting the others."

MATTHEW 23: 23 (HCSB)

DIRECTION FOR TODAY:

Are you a faithful steward of money or are there areas where you have allowed it to control you?

_____

_____

_____

_____

_____

_____

_____

_____

STUPID AND IGNORANT

ARE YOUR DAILY ACTIVITIES STILL CREATIVE AND STIMULATING OR HAVE YOU FALLEN INTO A REPETITIVE TRAP?

While driving through the Cotswolds of England on a family vacation, I was reminded of the simple kinds of work still being done by the people there. Many of them raise sheep, shear the wool, and barter with neighbors for products and services they need. Their houses are quaint, with charming personalities, yet simple and utilitarian. In early evening they may meet with friends at the local pub for fish, chips, peas, and a little ale. Their lives seem to be uncomplicated, varied and full of meaningful family times.

In the rapid growth of the industrialized United States, we have confused bigger with better, more work with more *"success"* and in the process lost many simple pleasures. Often our work is little more than a paycheck—and may fall into a boring, repetitive process, long since devoid of challenge and appealing engagement.

"The world will never be happy until all men have the souls of an artist –I mean when they take pleasure in their jobs." — **Auguste Rodin**

As far back as 1776, Adam Smith saw the dangers of moving in this direction. In his highly influential **Wealth of Nations**, he wrote that a person who spends his life performing the same repetitive tasks tends to lose *"the habit of exertion"* and *"generally becomes as stupid and ignorant as it is possible for a human creature to become."* Wow—now that's not a pretty picture. Unfortunately, much of our "work" in this country has moved us toward those boring, repetitive tasks. If your daily tasks could be completed by a trained monkey, watch out. You are at risk not only of brain deadness; you also are highly at risk for being replaced.

"All men of action are dreamers." — **James G. Huneker**

Here are some questions you might ask yourself:

Do you admire your boss and the philosophy of the company?

Do you identify with the products or services that your company provides?

Is your work using your best talents?

Are your spouse and children proud of the work you are doing?

Are you where you thought you'd be at this stage of your life?

Yes, it requires challenge to keep our creative natures engaged, but where there is no challenge there is a clear danger of stagnation or arrested development.

FROM THE BIBLE:

"A man can do nothing better than to eat and drink and find satisfaction in his work. This too, I see, is from the hand of God, for without Him, who can eat or find enjoyment? To the man who pleases Him, God gives wisdom, knowledge and happiness, but to the sinner He gives the task of gathering and storing up wealth to hand it over to the one who pleases God."

ECCLESIASTES 3: 24-26 (HCSB)

DIRECTION FOR TODAY:

What do people say about your work? How do you describe your work to others?

_____

_____

_____

_____

_____

BUT I CAN'T DO THAT

ARE THE BARRIERS YOU SEE REAL, OR SIMPLE BOUNDARIES THAT EXIST ONLY IN YOUR MIND?

On May 6, 1954, Roger Bannister ran the first sub-four-minute mile in recorded history. Doctors said it could not be done—that the human heart would explode with such exertion. Six weeks later an Australian runner duplicated that feat. Approximately one year later, 8 college runners at one ACAA track meet all broke the four-minute mile. What changed? Did humans suddenly evolve to be faster than ever before in history? Not likely. What did happen is that the level of expectation changed. What was believed to be impossible was proven to be possible. Most of us operate under clear beliefs about what we are able to accomplish. If those beliefs are changed, the results change as well.

Zig Ziglar tells his famous story about *flea training*. As he tells it so convincingly, if you put fleas in a jar with a lid on it, they will desperately pop up against that lid in an attempt to escape—for about 20 minutes. Then, while fully convinced they cannot get out of the top of that jar, you can remove the lid. With a perfectly clear path to freedom, those little fleas will starve to death in that jar. They tried it once and they *believe* there is no other option. I find many people living their lives within boundaries that exist only in their minds.

What artificial barrier have you placed in your life? Are you telling yourself that you are not intelligent enough to finish college, or you're not deserving enough to get a better job, or not pretty enough to find a mate, or don't have enough money to take your family on vacation? Are you convinced that something is impossible for you or out of your reach? Is it really out of reach or could it possibly just be your level of belief?

"To know what you prefer instead of humbly saying 'Amen' to what the world tells you you ought to prefer, is to have kept your soul alive."

— **Robert Louis Stevenson**

If you don't think you are the best candidate for a new job, do you think the company will convince you that you are? If you don't think you can climb a mountain, do you think you will ever get to the top? No, it never happens that way. If you can't see yourself achieving a new goal, believe me, it never will happen. Ask any athlete who wins an event and you'll find they believed they could before it really happened.

"Make no small plans; they have no magic to stir men's souls."

—**Daniel Burnam**

FROM THE BIBLE:

". . . I tell you the truth, if you have faith as small as a mustard seed, you can say to this mountain, 'Move from here to there' and it will move. Nothing will be impossible for you."

MATTHEW 17: 20 (NIV)

DIRECTION FOR TODAY:

What have you been telling yourself you could not accomplish? What can you do to make it happen?

_____

_____

_____

_____

_____

_____

_____

_____

Don't Chase The Snake

Don't waste your energy fretting about what has already happened—what are you doing tomorrow?

When I was 10 years old, one of my best friends was Bob Queen. One afternoon while exploring the back acreage of our neighboring farms, a snake bit Bob. Seeing the snake slither off, my immediate response was to run after the snake, track him down and repay the scoundrel for what he had done to my friend. Bob, however, being a much wiser hunter and outdoorsman, quickly pulled out his knife, lanced the bite, sucked the blood out and spit out the poison. The focus for him was on his own well being, not on repaying the snake.

> *Losers focus on what they are going through; Champions focus on what they are going to.*
> **—Dr. Mike Murdock**

How often I see people chasing the snake in their own lives. The company folds or you just simply get laid off. The immediate reaction may include anger, resentment, bitterness, and backstabbing. These lead to discouragement, frustration, guilt and depression. Be aware that all of these reactions and feelings focus on the past. Turning around and looking to the future opens up confidence, boldness, and enthusiasm. These often lead to an increased sense of accomplishment, personal control, fulfillment and even money.

> *"Live out of your imagination, not your history."*
> **— Stephen Covey**

I once worked with a client who had been with her company for over 22 years. She was paid in excess of $300,000 annually and had a long list of accomplishments. However, with new management they had demoted her, moved her from her corner office and dramatically reduced her responsibilities. She had recently received a negative performance review. It doesn't take a rocket scientist to see that they were moving her out—and quickly. She was experiencing stomach pains, high blood pressure and increased fatigue. Even though she had received several very attractive offers from sister companies, her first response was to defend her position, request meetings with the new CEO and futilely attempt to regain what would never be the same again. My advice—quit chasing the snake.

"Though no one can go back and make a brand new start, anyone can start from now and make a brand new ending."

— Carl Bard

If Bob and I had chased that snake, the poison would have been given opportunity to plunge through his veins, draining his energy and perhaps leading to his death. What are you doing in your life? Are you chasing a snake in the past or pursuing a dream in the future? Choose carefully; your life may be at stake.

FROM THE BIBLE:

"Obey me and I will be your God and you shall be my people; only do as I say and all shall be well! But they wouldn't listen; they kept on doing whatever they wanted to, following their own stubborn, evil thoughts. They went backward instead of forward."

JEREMIAH 7: 23-24 (TLB)

DIRECTION FOR TODAY:

What snake have you been chasing? What decisions can you make to go forward with confidence, boldness and enthusiasm?

_____

_____

_____

Are You A Genius

Do you find solutions no one else can find or are you just "smart?"

In 1904, Havelock Ellis noted that most geniuses were fathered by men older than 30, had mothers younger than 25, and usually were sickly children. Other researchers have reported that many were celibate (Descartes), fatherless (Dickens), or motherless (Darwin). The bottom line is that the research and data are not at all consistent. There is also no correlation between genius and intelligence. Genius does not appear to be about scoring 1600 on your SAT, mastering quantum physics at age 7, or even being especially smart.

Rather, genius seems to be about being able to see solutions that others don't see. The mark of genius is being willing to explore all the alternatives, not just the most likely solution. Asked to describe the difference between himself and an average person, Albert Einstein explained that the average person faced with the problem of finding a needle in a haystack would stop when he/she found a needle. But Einstein would tear through the entire haystack looking for all possible needles.

> *"We should take care not to make the intellect our god; it has of course powerful muscles, but no personality. It cannot lead, it can only serve."*
>
> **— Leonardo da Vinci**

Seeking to approach the usual in an unusual way can often lead to new solutions. Purposeful, principled dissent can offer us *"perspective by incongruity"*. In mythology, the Greek god Janus had two opposing faces, from which we get the term Janusian thinking. Being able to see things from two totally opposite viewpoints is often the beginning of genius thinking. Niels Bohr, a noted physicist, argues that if you hold opposites together in your mind, you will suspend your normal thinking process and allow an intelligence beyond rational thought to create a new form. Our society tells us to stay inside the lines. God gives us a blank sheet of paper and infinite creativity.

The real act of discovery is not in finding new lands, but in seeing with new eyes.
— **Marcel Proust**

Now, what about that job search? Are you going to look at the newspaper classifieds like the thousands of others looking for work or are you going to do something different? I had a client once who sent his introduction letters out, wrapped around an ear of corn and then used a play on that for his message— *"Aw, shucks, I'm sure you think this is corny, but just give me your ear for a minute,"* etc. etc. Yes, he got response and immediate opportunities. Are you a genius or are you just another smart, intelligent, sophisticated, high IQ, great GPA, predictable, lacking results kind of person?

FROM THE BIBLE:

"How does a man become wise? The first step is to trust and reverence the Lord! Only fools refuse to be taught."

PROVERBS 1:7-8 (TLB)

DIRECTION FOR TODAY:

How can you broaden the options for solutions on a problem you have today?

_____

_____

_____

_____

_____

_____

Just Doing My Job

Doing a job does not justify compromises in integrity, character or values.

Henry David Thoreau once said: *"A man had better starve at once than lose his innocence in the process of getting his bread."* Just doing a job cannot justify doing something unethical, immoral, or dishonest. The guards in the German concentration camps, after becoming friends with the prisoners, would often justify walking them to the gas chambers with, *"I'm just doing my job."*

Unfortunately, I still see people who are selling cars they know are defective, products they can't deliver, food they know is rotten, Florida resort land that is nothing but swamp, dental work that isn't really needed, financial figures that are not quite accurate, and *"business opportunities"* that don't really work. What is it that you can justify doing just because it's part of your job? Just because you have the ability to do something well is not enough reason to continue doing it—if it violates your values and common sense.

We are in a culture that separates *"work"* from the rest of our *"life."* Even American Christians seem to live by the premise that being Christian effects what we do on Sundays, but the rest of the week—well, that's just our work. This is an artificial dichotomy. Our work is our life and a clearer expression of who we are than what we do on any given Sunday.

> **"The measure of a man is not what he does on Sunday, but rather who he is Monday through Saturday."**

In the Hebrew language there was a word, *"avodah"* from which we get both our words, *"work"* and *"worship."* To them there was no distinction. What a person was doing on Thursday morning was just as much an expression of worship or lack thereof as being in the synagogue on the Sabbath. Our work is a form of our worship.

"Work is love made visible. And if you cannot work with love but only with distaste, it is better that you should leave your work and sit at the gate of the temple and take alms of those who work with joy.

For if you bake bread with indifference, you bake a bitter bread that feeds but half man's hunger.

And if you grudge the crushing of the grapes, your grudge distills a poison in the wine."

—Kahil Gibran, from "The Prophet"

If your work doesn't express your values, you're setting yourself up for deceit in other areas of your life. And for the invasion of ulcers, migraines and cancer as evidence of a less than authentic life. In the movie *Cool Hand Luke*, a guard says, *"I'm just doing my job. You gotta appreciate that."* And Paul Newman responds: *"Nah, Calling it your job don't make it right, boss."* I agree.

FROM THE BIBLE:

"Don't work for food that perishes but for the good that lasts for eternal life...."

JOHN 6: 27 (HCSB)

DIRECTION FOR TODAY:

Is your "job" an expression of worship for you? If not, what can you do to change it?

_____

_____

_____

_____

_____

_____

Jobs Come and Go — But Beauty and Grace Continue

Don't allow circumstances to blind you to the richness of life all around you.

There are two bluebird families making nests outside my window this morning. The chickadees are moving into a newly hung birdhouse as well. A brave groundhog just ambled from our barn to the wooded area along the fence.

Yes, work needs to be done, plans need to be made, but have you noticed the beauty around you today? In 1988, I experienced a major business failure. Our business was sold at auction, leaving us thousands and thousands of dollars in debt. The IRS demanded the immediate sale of our house and cars and seized that money. I recognized that I was a sitting duck for negativism and *"victim"* thinking to fill my mind and day. I began a routine of spending at least two hours a day reading and listening to positive, uplifting material. Add to that a loving wife, supportive friends, a strong Christian faith, and my own motivation, and I was able to begin the long road back to increased success in all areas of my life.

Job, career or business failures often precipitate a spiraling down in areas beyond just money. Job loss creates immediate financial pressure, leading to relationship strain. This lowers self-esteem, reduces motivation for physical and personal development. Faith is often questioned —- If there is a God who cares why did this happen to me?

"Life is made of moments, small pieces of glittering mica in a long stretch of gray cement. It would be wonderful if they came to us unsummoned, but particularly in lives as busy as the ones most of us lead now, that won't happen. We have to teach ourselves how to live, really live...to love the journey, not the destination."

—**Anna Quindlen**

Make daily success deposits in those areas you can control. If the rent is due and you just got turned down once more in a job interview, you can still decide to love your kids and go for an invigorating walk. One night last week, I turned the lights off in our living room, called Joanne in to join me, and we sat on the couch and just watched the moon travel across the sky.

> *"Beauty and grace are performed whether or not we will sense them. The least we can do is try to be there . . . so that creation need not play to an empty house."*
> —(Annie Dillard in *"Pilgrim at Tinker Creek"*)

Don't miss the richest pleasures available to you whether or not you have a job you love. Enjoying the simple things will add to your clarity about what work fits you well.

FROM THE BIBLE:

"I will lift up mine eyes unto the hills, from whence cometh my help. My help cometh from the Lord, which made heaven and earth."

PSALM 121: 1-2 (KJV)

DIRECTION FOR TODAY:

What are three unique examples of beauty and grace that you have already recognized in your life today?

_____

_____

_____

_____

_____

_____

"Cow Paths" and Water Buffalo Thinking

Expected familiarity does not necessarily lead us to the best options and opportunities.

I grew up on a farm and had plenty of time to practice my *"success"* principles on our cows. Unfortunately, they were not good examples of creative thinking and innovation, but rather, were easy to confuse and control. Scientists have described the standard, unchallenged thinking of humans as *"cow paths in the brain."* Cows will all follow each other, usually in a single line, moving along in a very predictable pattern. They do not challenge this pattern, even when it is clearly self-defeating. If an obstacle appears, they will stay where they are, waiting for the obstacle to be removed.

When we were young children, no *"paths"* existed. We took in and processed information in all parts of our brains with seemingly endless options as possibilities. However, as we grew from infancy to childhood and beyond, our brains developed identifiable paths. We no longer used our whole brain as we learned to limit the options we would consider.

> *"The difficulty lies not so much in developing new ideas as in escaping from old ones."*
>
> **—John Maynard Keynes**

Chauncey M. Depew confessed that he warned his nephew not to invest five thousand dollars in Ford stock because *"nothing has come along to beat the horse."* Charles H. Duell, commissioner of the U.S. Patent Office, urged President William McKinley to abolish the patent office in 1899 because *"everything that can be invented has been invented."* Experts predicted that the introduction of the railroad would require the building of many insane asylums as people would be driven mad with terror at the sight of locomotives rushing across the country.

Each of us have *"cow paths"* that keep us from seeing all there is to see. We limit ourselves by not looking for the real opportunities available to us. Phrases like *"everybody's laying off"* or *"nobody's hiring"* or *"I don't have enough money to start my own business"* or *"I'm too old"* are examples of *"cow path"* thinking.

"A lot of what we think of as neurosis in this country is simply people who are unhappy because they're not using their creative resources."

—Julia Cameron

If you're feeling trapped or you just stepped in something mushy or you think the whole world stinks, it's likely that you are simply on a *"cow path."* Move off that path and you may see a whole new field of opportunity.

FROM THE BIBLE:

"With men it is impossible, but not with God, because all things are possible with God."

MARK 10: 27 (HCSB

DIRECTION FOR TODAY:

What are two examples of "cow path" thinking you suspect in your life today? How can you break out of those?

_____

_____

_____

_____

_____

_____

MY LIFE IS LIKE A BAMBOO TREE

THE RESULTS OF DOING THINGS RIGHT MAY NOT BE EVIDENT IMMEDIATELY, BUT KEEP WATERING ANYWAY!

Hey, I'm like all of you. I want it all NOW! We have grown up in a culture that expects instant everything—so we use microwaves, cell phones, fax machines, TV dinners, and email. However, much to our chagrin, most important things still take time. Relationships, kindness, prayer, leisure, rejuvenation, creativity and imagination require *time* for their development.

I like the story of the Chinese bamboo tree: You take a little seed, plant it, water it, and fertilize it for a whole year, and nothing happens. The second year you water it and fertilize it, and nothing happens. The third year you water it and fertilize it, and nothing happens. How discouraging this becomes! The fifth year you continue to water and fertilize the seed and then—-take note. Sometime during the fifth year, the Chinese bamboo tree sprouts and grows NINETY FEET IN SIX WEEKS!

> *"The greatest thing in this world is not so much where we are, but in what direction we are moving."*
>
> **—Oliver Wendell Holmes**

Life is much like the growing process of the Chinese bamboo tree. It is often discouraging. We seemingly do things right, and nothing happens. But for those who do things right and are not discouraged and are persistent, things will happen. Finally we begin to receive the rewards.

For more than 5 years I counseled hundreds of people in career issues as a volunteer care-giver through our local church. When I then launched a full-time life coaching business, the referrals from all those earlier people overflowed my schedule from the first opening day. Phenomenal success in marketing early *"self-published"* career planning training manuals now bring major publishers my way as willing partners. The excitement I still experience in my marriage is due to making deposits for success over many years. The vibrant health I enjoy is certainly due in part to daily habits of good nutrition, meditation, and exercise for much more than just five years.

"It is not enough to be busy; so are the ants. The question is: What are we busy about?"

— **Henry David Thoreau**

I am now receiving the rewards of seeds that were planted 5 years ago. You are as well. Are you getting the results you want? If not, begin today to sow the seeds of what you want 5 years from now. Remember, if you keep doing what you've always done, you'll get the results you've always gotten.

FROM THE BIBLE:

". . . Make every effort to supplement your faith with goodness, goodness with knowledge, knowledge with self-control, self-control with endurance, endurance with godliness, godliness with brotherly affection, and brotherly affection with love. For if these qualities are yours and are increasing, they will keep you from being useless or unfruitful in the knowledge of our Lord Jesus Christ."

II Peter 1: 5-8 (HCSB)

DIRECTION FOR TODAY:

What are three things you can do today to make success deposits for where you want to be five years from now?

_____

_____

_____

_____

SMILE OR GO HOME

YOUR FACE MAY TELL MORE ABOUT YOU THAN YOUR RESUME.

I had the privilege of meeting Dave Anderson, founder of **Famous Dave's BBQ** restaurants at a conference for writers. Soon thereafter, Joanne and I visited the only **Famous Dave's** in the Nashville area. We were greeted enthusiastically, taken to our table and wowed by the young lady who would be our server. She explained that she would be checking on us continually to make sure our experience there was a memorable one. Then the manager came by. We commented on the atmosphere and the attitude of all the staff. He grinned and explained, *"If they aren't smiling, I send them home."* The rest of the duties were secondary to that one simple requirement.

There is an old Chinese saying that goes something like this: *"A man without a smiling face must not open a shop."* I guess Dave Anderson knows that principle. Another restaurant here in our market area shouts when you open the door, *"Welcome to Moe's!"* The menu items are good but the real lasting impression is of that welcome greeting when you walk in the door. Guess where we like to take our guests when they're in town?

A Yale University study shows that only 15% of a person's success is due to technical skill, intelligence, degrees, certification, etc.—those things we can measure. 85% is due to personal skills—attitude, enthusiasm, tone of voice, honesty, smile, etc.

That same phenomenon has much the same effect on interviewers. In a survey conducted among 5000 human resource managers, one of the questions was: *"What do you look for most in a candidate?"* Of the 2756 who responded, 2322 ranked enthusiasm first. The first thing interviewers look for in a candidate is vitality and enthusiasm. Many candidates with the right background experience and skills disqualify themselves with a demeanor that suggests they lack energy.

The easiest way to convey energy and enthusiasm is to smile. Now there's a tip that you can implement today. No waiting, no paying for expensive degrees, no buying a new suit—just smile!!

In the classic little book, *"The Magic of Thinking Big,"* David Schwartz challenges the readers with this test. *"Try to feel defeated and smile big at the same time. You can't. A big smile gives you confidence. A big smile beats fear, rolls away worry, defeats despondency."*

Hey, here's a complicated theory — If you want a raise or better job opportunities, want to make a lasting impression or just make more friends, try smiling more.

FROM THE BIBLE:

"When a man is gloomy, everything seems to go wrong; when he is cheerful, everything seems right."

PROVERBS 15:15 (TLB)

DIRECTION FOR TODAY:

What will your face tell people about the condition of your heart today?

_____

_____

_____

_____

_____

_____

_____

_____

_____

_____

COOKED IN THE SQUAT

SOMETIMES MORE KNOWLEDGE BRINGS CONFUSION RATHER THAN CLARITY.

Most of us make fun of the idea that ignorance is bliss and pride ourselves in not being one of the ignorant. However, I see a reverse phenomenon that is also quite interesting. The paradox of knowledge is this: the more we know, the more we realize what we don't know. Thus, a person who begins studying butterflies discovers the thousands of species that exist. A person who wants to buy a car can get lost in consumer reports, safety studies, and resale potential. I see students continuing the pursuit of more and more degrees, *"getting ready"* for that first job. I see people looking for a job who spend six months researching companies and job search strategies. I encounter the frustrated employee who wants his/her own business and spends ten years carefully planning every possible outcome.

> *"Action may not always bring happiness, but there is no happiness without action."*
> —**Benjamin Disraeli**

One of Zig Ziglar's famous stories is of a childhood neighbor lady who pulled some biscuits out of the oven that were no thicker than silver dollars. When little Zig asked what happened, the cook laughed and said, *"Well, those biscuits squatted to rise, but they just got cooked in the squat."*

I see people who have gotten *"cooked in the squat."* They are going to do something just as soon as they gather all the necessary information. But weeks, months and then years slip by. Protected in the safety of gathering more information they miss new opportunities all together. A client told me he had gone to work at the local bank—just as a temporary position until he could do a little research about which career field to really pursue. Guess what? That was 17 years ago and he's still at the bank. The acceptable illusion of still getting ready robbed him of 17 years of his life.

"You don't have to be great to get started, but you have to get started to be great."
— Les Brown

When do you have enough knowledge to start something new? **When you decide to take action!** The baby eagle learns how to fly as he is heading straight toward the rocks below, not while sitting on the edge of the nest. The business owner learns while hiring, buying, and making mistakes more than while sitting in a classroom. The unemployed person approaches success while knocking on doors, making phone calls, and getting repeated rejections, not while scanning the Internet and reading textbooks.

"There is no more miserable human being than the one in whom nothing is habitual but indecision."

—William James

Don't get *"cooked in the squat."* It will cripple you!

FROM THE BIBLE:

"And further, by these, my son, be admonished: of making many books there is no end; and much study is a weariness of the flesh."

ECCLESIASTES 12: 12 (KJV)

DIRECTION FOR TODAY:

What is a decision you are waiting to make? Do you perhaps have enough "knowledge" to make a decision and move on?

_____

_____

_____

_____

_____

THE MEXICAN FISHERMAN

SOMETIMES "SUCCESS" IS SEEING WHAT WE
ALREADY HAVE IN A NEW LIGHT.

An American businessman was at the pier of a small coastal Mexican village when a small boat with just one fisherman docked. Inside the small boat were several large yellow fin tuna. The American complimented the Mexican on the quality of his fish and asked how long it took to catch them.

The Mexican replied, *"Only a little while."* The American then asked why he didn't stay out longer and catch more fish. The Mexican said he had enough to support his family's immediate needs.

The American then asked, *"But what do you do with the rest of your time?"*

The Mexican fisherman said, *"I sleep late, fish a little, play with my children, take a siesta with my wife, Maria, stroll into the village each evening where I sip wine and play guitar with my amigos. I have a full and busy life."*

The American scoffed, *"I'm a Harvard MBA and I could help you. You should spend more time fishing and with the proceeds buy a bigger boat. With the proceeds from the bigger boat you could buy several boats, eventually you would have a fleet of fishing boats. Instead of selling your catch to a middleman you would sell directly to the processor, eventually opening your own cannery. You would control the product, processing and distribution. You would need to leave this small coastal fishing village and move to Mexico City, then LA and eventually NYC where you will run your expanding enterprise."*

The Mexican fisherman asked, *"But, how long will all this take?"* To which the American replied, *"15-20 years." "But what then?"* The American laughed and said, *"That's the best part. When the time is right you would announce an IPO and sell your company stock to the public and become very rich. You would make millions."*

"Millions? Then what?" the native fisherman asked. *"Then you could retire. Move to a small coastal fishing village where you would sleep late, fish a little, play with your kids,*

take a siesta with your wife, and stroll to the village in the evenings where you could sip wine and play your guitar with your amigos." *

"And in the end, it's not the years in your life that count. It's the life in your years."
— Abraham Lincoln

*I've borrowed from this story that's been circulating in many forms—original Author Unknown

---

FROM THE BIBLE:

". . . I have learned to be content whatever the circumstances. I know what it is to be in need, and I know what it is to have plenty. I have learned the secret of being content in any and every situation, whether well fed or hungry, whether living in plenty or in want."

PHILIPPIANS 4:11-12 (NIV)

DIRECTION FOR TODAY:

Do you really need to build bigger barns or have you been overlooking the real success you already have?

_____

_____

_____

_____

_____

_____

LOOKING AROUND BUT FEELING DOWN

NEGATIVE ATTITUDES WILL KEEP YOU LIVING IN YOUR LOSS—RATHER THAN MOVING TOWARD NEW GAIN.

Losing a job can lead to anger, resentment, guilt and depression. I once worked with a gentleman who having lost his job, tried to reposition himself and do a job search, only to become discouraged after just a few days with no success. He was hiding out from his wife, pretending to be doing a job search, while in reality he was going to the library to surf the Internet and read magazines. He consoled himself in fast food and high sugar snacks and quickly added about 25 pounds. This, in turn, made him self-conscious about his weight and ill-fitting clothes. *"I hated my job, but am still angry about being let go,"* he said.

> *"The greatest test of courage on earth is to bear defeat without losing heart."*
> — **Robert G. Ingersoll, US lawyer, orator**

This story is not unusual. New research confirms that losing a job can put people at an elevated risk for emotional and physical problems. Unemployment can start a vicious cycle of depression, loss of personal discipline and decreased emotional health. *"Depression can contribute to much longer searches,"* notes John Challenger, CEO of outplacement firm Challenger, Gray & Christmas.

> *"Every action we take, everything we do, is either a victory or defeat in the struggle to become what we want to be."*
> — **Anne Byrhhe, US educator**

Failure in a business, the dissolution of a relationship, a breakdown of health, or a financial disaster can also be a set-up for these negative, self-defeating feelings. Any of these situations can make a person a candidate for the downward spiral of anger, resentment, guilt and depression.

"They say when one door of happiness closes, another opens. But the problem is... we look so long at the closed door that we never notice the open one."

To break the cycle, take charge of the areas where you can experience immediate success. Increase physical exercise—and note the satisfaction of increased vitality and creative thinking. Increase volunteering and feel the rewards of offering a helping hand. Increase positive reading and listening to inspiring audio tapes—and find yourself with new thinking and ideas. Do special things for loved ones—and feel their genuine support and encouragement. Give thanks for the things you do have. The best fuel for a negative attitude is an ungrateful heart. Recognize the wonderful things you do have—rather than focusing on the area of lack in your life. We can give thanks IN all circumstances—not FOR them, but IN them.

None of these are directly related to getting a new job, starting another business, rebuilding your health, or finding another friend and yet they are very much related. From these actions come the boldness, confidence and enthusiasm necessary to nurture the success you are seeking.

FROM THE BIBLE:

"Be joyful always; pray continually; give thanks in all circumstances, for this is God's will for you in Christ Jesus."

I Thessalonians 5: 18 (NIV)

DIRECTION FOR TODAY:

In what area of your life are negative feelings holding you back?

_____

_____

_____

SLEEPING IN THE BUS

TIME SPENT IN ONLY ONE AREA OF YOUR LIFE WILL ROB SUCCESS FROM OTHER IMPORTANT AREAS.

Willie Nelson has been known to do 200-plus gigs a year. Traveling in the "Honeysuckle Rose," Willie connects with his audience in a way that few performers ever do. This little 70+year-old pigtailed guy from Abbot, Texas was picked to lead the singing of "America the Beautiful" on the worldwide broadcast of a relief benefit for the victims of 9/11. He has also raised over $23 million for struggling family farms.

However, this kind of *"success"* comes with a high personal price. Lacking balance in personal areas, Willie has wife number 4 and 7 children who rarely see him. Willie's fourth wife, Annie, lives with their two sons, Lukas, 14, and Micah, 12, in Maui; Willie gets there *"when he can."*

Even when Willie is back at his fabulous Austin, TX compound — which includes a recording studio, golf course, and Western film set—he still lives on the bus. Neither this compound nor his place in Maui is home—the bus is.

If you are working more than 50-60 hours a week on your job or business, you're probably spending too much time on *"the bus."* Success in family, physical, spiritual, social, and personal development requires an investment of your time. *"On the road again"* makes for a fine country song but it will strangle your ultimate success in life.

"There is a pervasive form of contemporary violence . . . (and that is) activism and overwork.

The rush and pressure of modern life are a form, perhaps the most common form, of its innate violence."

—Thomas Merton

In my work as a life coach I have seen people from every career and professional area. I have seen pastors who are working 80 hours a week, justifying it because it's doing *"the Lords work."* Physicians justify long hours because they are *"helping people."* Landscapers justify long hours because their *"work is seasonal."* Painters work under night lights because *"I've got to pay the bills."* It's easy to rationalize *"living on the bus"* whether we are singing songs, saving souls or fixing leaky faucets. Prayer, tenderness, intimacy, kindness—all these things thrive in rest, and not in speed.

In the popular book, *7 Habits of Highly Effective People*, Steven Covey laid out those seven important practices. Remember the principle of *"sharpening the saw?"* If you are always relentlessly pursuing your dream you may just be getting a dull blade. Thomas Edison went fishing each morning—throwing a line in without any bait. But it was his best time for creative thinking and coming up with new inventions.

FROM THE BIBLE:

"Be still, and know that I am God."

Psalm 46: 10 (KJV)

DIRECTION FOR TODAY:

Have you been guilty of "sleeping on the bus?" How has that affected other areas of your life in negative ways?

_____

_____

_____

_____

_____

_____

_____

_____

UNEMPLOYMENT - WHAT'S THAT

ARE TIMES IN BETWEEN "JOBS" WASTED? IS OUR WORTH DEFINED ONLY BY WHAT WE DO?

Do you know that in the Tibetan language there is no word for *"unemployment?"* That is a concept reserved for our Western culture where we have *"jobs."* In traditional Tibetan society, people were mostly farmers, animal herders, or merchants. There was no concept of set hours of work or of having a job. Their work was often seasonal and during harvest season, they would work very hard. Then during the off season, they and the land would rest.

That pattern of natural work and rest has been replaced in our culture with 24/7 accessibility to work. Cell phones ring in church, email arrives at 2:00 AM demanding a response, and faxes peel off pages of urgent business in family kitchens. We have created artificial environments with artificial work expectations.

> *"Happiness is a butterfly, which, when pursued, is always just beyond your grasp, but which, if you will sit down quietly, may alight upon you."*
> —Nathaniel Hawthorne (1804-1864)

We also attach a great deal of meaning to our jobs. Thus, if the job disappears, the immediate response can be that of diminished self-worth and clouded identity. A person without a "job" is assumed to be a life on hold. I have seen thousands of clients struggle with these inevitable transitions—hiding out to keep neighbors or friends from knowing the truth. If we have no identity apart from our jobs, we are truly vulnerable.

> *A gem cannot be polished without friction, nor people perfected without trials.*
> —Chinese Proverb

I guess that's why I look back and value being raised on a farm where the sun and rain often dictated the day's activities. I love the convenience of modern technology, but as with all *"advancements"* there also comes the responsibility for maintaining personal life balance. Self-worth comes from meaningful time spent in reading a good book, in walking hand-in-hand with a spouse through a park, in teaching a child to ride a bike, or in volunteering for a Habitat for Humanity project.

> *"God respects me when I work, but he loves me when I sing."*　　　—Rumi

I have always encouraged people to recognize times of being *"between opportunities."* Rather than the panic of being off-track, on hold, or *"unemployed,"* perhaps we should see those times as welcome times of restoration, rejuvenation and opportunities for new perspective. Seeing it as such would certainly require a new word. Any ideas?

FROM THE BIBLE:

"So don't worry, saying 'What will we eat?' or 'What will we drink?' or 'What will we wear?'. . . But seek first the kingdom of God and His righteousness, and all these things will be provided for you."

MATTHEW 6: 31, 33 (HCSB)

DIRECTION FOR TODAY:

What are three things that give you a sense of worth—outside of your job?

_____

_____

_____

_____

_____

_____

DID YOU LOSE YOUR HORSE TODAY

"IS LOSING MY JOB, INCOME, BUSINESS OR HEALTH A BLESSING OR A CURSE?"

Once there was an old man who lived in a tiny village. Although poor, he was envied by all, because he owned a beautiful white horse. People offered fabulous prices for the horse, but the old man always refused. *"This horse is a friend, not a possession,"* he would respond.

One morning the horse was not in the stable. All the villagers said, *"You old fool. We told you someone would steal that beautiful horse. You could at least have gotten the money. Now the horse is gone, and you've been cursed with misfortune."* The old man responded, *"Perhaps. All I know is that my horse is gone; the rest I do not know. Whether it be a curse or a blessing, I can't say."*

After fifteen days the horse returned. He hadn't been stolen; he had run away into the forest. Not only had he returned, he had brought a dozen wild horses back with him. Once again the village people gathered around the old man and said, *"You were right—what we thought was a curse was a blessing. Please forgive us."* The old man responded, *"Perhaps. Once again you've gone too far. How do you know if this is a blessing or a curse? Unless you can see the whole story, how can you judge?"* But the people could only see the obvious. The old man now had twelve additional horses that could be broken and sold for a great deal of money.

The old man had a son, an only son. He began to break the wild horses. Unfortunately, after just a few days, he fell from a horse and broke both his legs. Once again the villagers gathered around the old man and said, *"You were right. The wild horses were not a blessing; they were a curse. Your only son has broken his legs and now in your old age you have no one to help you. You are poorer than ever."* But the old man said, *"Perhaps. Don't go so far. Say only that my son broke his legs. We have only a fragment of the whole story."*

It so happened that a few weeks later the country went to war with a neighboring country. All the young men of the village were required to join the army. Only the son of the old man was excluded, because he had two broken legs. Once again the people gathered around, crying because there was little chance their sons would return. *"You were right, old man."* Your son's accident was a blessing. Our sons are gone forever."

The old man spoke again. *"You people are always quick to jump to conclusions. Only God knows the final story."*

(I have modified the details of this story that I've seen in various forms in many sources. No author has been identified.)

FROM THE BIBLE:

"No eye has seen, no ear has heard, no mind has conceived what God has prepared for those who love him."

I CORINTHIANS 2: 9 (NIV)

DIRECTION FOR TODAY:

Is there something in your life today that others would consider a curse? Is it really?

_____

_____

_____

_____

_____

_____

_____

_____

Let's Slay a Dragon

Have you created boundaries that don't really exist except in your own mind?

Centuries ago, when mapmakers drew all they knew of the world, they would sketch a dragon at the edge of the scroll. This was a sign to the explorer that beyond this, he would be entering unknown and perhaps dangerous territory. Unfortunately, many explorers took this symbol literally and refused to push out to new worlds. A few saw these dragons as a sign of opportunity, a door to places no one had gone before.

Each of us has a mental map of what we allow ourselves to explore. Like those maps of long ago, many of us see dragons and danger in going beyond our familiar territory. It may be a fear of computers, a fear of interviewing, the embarrassment of not having a college degree, or the panic of being in front of people.

> *"If a man harbors any sort of fear, it percolates through all his thinking, damages his personality, makes him a landlord to a ghost."*
>
> **—Lloyd C. Douglas**

Ron came to me for life coaching. At 39, he had never owned a house, had never been married, had never traveled outside the United States and been in the same boring job for 17 years. He longed to have a family and to do something more meaningful in his work. But the imagined dragons inherent in the risk of trying new things kept him trapped in his very narrow and safe world. As we laid out conservative but definite plans for action in each of these areas he became energized, confident and enthusiastic. Today he has several real estate investments, is a leader on his church missions' trips to Central America and is involved in a romantic relationship that appears headed for marriage. He's even thinking about buying a sports car.

"Never take counsel of your fears."   —**Andrew Jackson**

Let's slay a dragon today! What if you purposely took on one of those uncharted territories? Could you get another degree this year? Could you find a way to double your income? Could you learn a new language—join Toastmasters, or make 5 new friends? Could you start your own business, travel to Spain, learn how to interview effectively, or go to an art class?

Guess what? Dragons don't really exist except as we allow them to. Our fears are usually exaggerated—once you step up to the plate you may realize that you were born to be the next great hitter.

Need help stretching your ideas? Check out *"48 Days To Creative Income"* or some of the other resources at: http://www.48days.com/products.php

---

FROM THE BIBLE:

"For he shall give his angels charge over thee, to keep thee in all thy ways. They shall bear thee up in their hands, lest thou dash thy foot against a stone. Thou shalt tread upon the lion and adder: the young lion and the dragon shalt thou trample under feet."

PSALM 91: 11-13 (KJV)

DIRECTION FOR TODAY:

What is the imaginary dragon that's holding you back today?

_____

_____

_____

_____

_____

HUMAN FILING CABINETS

OUR WORK ENVIRONMENTS DO CONTRIBUTE TO OUR SENSE OF VALUE AND PRODUCTIVITY.

I ran across this term in reference to office buildings — and it made my skin crawl. Much has been said about the depersonalization of the modern technology worker's work space. How can one be creative, innovative and contributing when in a work environment that has all the ambience of a veal-fattening pen?

Here's a piece from *"The Dilbert Principle,"* by Scott Adams:
Boss— *"We've got a lot of empty cubicles because of downsizing. I hired the Dogbert construction company to convert part of the office into prison cells which we'll lease to the state."*
Dilbert— *"Sounds like a big job."*
Boss— *"Nah, a little paint, new carpet and we're there."*

The cartoon continues to relate the differences in employees and prisoners; namely that the prisoners had a better health plan. And ultimately, the plan to use spare cubicles as prison cells had to be abandoned because of too many complaints from the prisoners.

I presented a workshop for one of the big telecommunications companies at their new facility. With pride, they gave me a tour of their new state-of-the art customer call center. There were approximately 300 cubicles in one gigantic warehouse. Yes, the colors were nice and you could see balloons where several employees had been rewarded for superior performance. But the lighting was dim and there was not a window in sight. After one short hour, that total artificial environment left me desperate to see sunshine and open spaces. Is there a subtle humiliation that keeps employees from being too self-confident or creative in this workplace? I remember back on the farm we used to raise chickens in the dark so they wouldn't see each other, interact or get any ideas about rebelling. I also got this funny picture in my mind about a game we used to play at the amusement park called, "Whack-a-Mole." Every time a mole popped his head up you would whack him on the head to get back down in his hole. I suspect there is an element of the same philosophy in the cubicle environment.

Work settings cannot be alienating and dehumanizing if we are to produce anything beyond what a machine could produce. Anything resembling *"Human Filing Cabinets"* will ultimately suck the life, energy and thinking intelligence out of those who succumb to that alternative.

FROM THE BIBLE:

"When I observe Your heavens, the work of Your fingers, the moon and the stars, which You set in place, what is man that You remember him, the son of man that You look after him? You made him a little less than God and crowned him with glory and honor. You made him lord over the works of Your hands; You put everything under his feet."

PSALM 8: 3-6 (HCSB)

DIRECTION FOR TODAY:

Is your work environment conducive to being most productive? If not, what could you do to improve it?

_____

_____

_____

_____

_____

_____

_____

Less Sleep, More Work — Maybe Not

Sufficient rest may be a prerequisite to productivity.

If you're like many serious career climbers today, you've relegated sleep to the bottom of your priority list, convincing yourself you can burn the midnight oil on your way to success instead.

We are in a culture that equates time with accomplishment. Thus we feel the constant pressure to work longer hours. The badge of honor is to be too busy. As we share how things are going, being busy beyond reason is a sure sign of success. Or is it? One of the clear by-products of this new economy where technology allows us 24/7 access to our workstations and instant information has been an almost total disregard for sleep, family and personal balance. The brightest and best appear to pride themselves on extreme commitment to work, ignoring relationships, and focusing on the business bottom line only.

I grew up on a farm, and in retrospect I see how successful my father really was. Yes, he worked hard, balancing the roles of both farmer and pastor. The pastorate paid nothing so the farm was our source of income and yet the duties of the pastorate always had equal priority. But the farming also forced a cycle of work and rest in that there were a few weeks of really hard work, but then the season ended or the rains came for a few days. Nothing could be done to alter these inevitable events of nature. I am convinced that God orchestrated the required periods of labor and restoration. And even with plenty of work to be done and with perfect weather conditions, Dad still recognized the power of *"keeping the Sabbath holy."*

Is giving up sleep the secret of success? Not according to James B. Maas, author of *"Power Sleep."* *"There is a way to condition yourself to get less sleep, but not to need less sleep,"* he contends. *"You're simply becoming habituated to a low level of alertness."* Maas believes if you get 8 hours of sleep, you will be able to get your 19 hours of work done in 12 efficient hours. Worried about missing *"success?"* Albert Einstein slept 10 hours a night.

There is more to life than increasing its speed.

—**Mohandas Gandhi**

My recommendation: Expect and make deposits for success in all areas of life, including physical, spiritual, and personal development. True desirable *"success"* does not come from 168 hours a week devoted to work. Find your level of needed sleep. Go to bed at a reasonable time and wake up when you are well rested.

FROM THE BIBLE:

"The Lord is my shepherd; there is nothing I lack. He lets me lie down in green pastures; He leads me beside quiet waters. He renews my life; He leads me along the right paths for His name's sake."

PSALM 23: 1-3 (HCSB)

DIRECTION FOR TODAY:

Are you getting your needed level of rest? Or are you functioning at a "low level of alertness?"

_____

_____

_____

_____

_____

_____

_____

I'm a Box Full of Parts That Don't Seem to Match

Finding a career focus is normally a long-term process—not a decision made by an 18 yr-old.

This is actually a quote from a career workshop attendee. The young man went on to describe how he had the ability to do a lot of things but had never found a clear focus for his career. In the spring of each year we always see a great number of college graduates who present the same feeling. *"Now that I have this degree, what am I supposed to do?"* Having a degree does not necessarily lead a person in a clear direction. That's why we know that 10 years after graduation, 80% of college graduates are working in something totally unrelated to their college degree.

Rather than being alarmed by this fact, we simply need to put the degree in perspective. A college degree is not intended to create a narrow career path from which there is no escape. In a broader sense it is part of the maturing process; it shows self-discipline; it expands one's horizons and options; it provides new social contacts; and it likely stimulates some possible career alternatives.

My own college degree was in psychology. The motivation for that had more to do with my desire for personal understanding than as a basis for a career. Five years after that degree I went back for a master's degree in clinical psychology. Then I sold cars, started an auto accessories business, bought a health and fitness center and consulted on small business issues. 18 years after that master's degree I began my doctoral program in religion and society. It was then, at about age 42 that I began to assimilate my academic and life experience into the most effective application—life coaching. I did not have the necessary personal experience or knowledge prior to that time to relate to the struggles of the inevitable transitions most of us travel through.

A person is not old until regrets take the place of dreams. **—John Barrymore**

Career choices are not for the most part logical and rational—the good ones are much more intuitive and clarified by life experience. That's why those of you who are already 35-40+ are in a better position to make good career decisions. What you have done in the real world has been preparing you to make clearer, more meaningful decisions than what you could possibly have done at age 18-20. Career decisions made at 18 seldom define the most fulfilling options 20 years later. Life is the ultimate educational experience that helps us make good decisions. And keep in mind that academic institutions are often safe, socially acceptable places to hide out while procrastinating having to make real choices.

Enjoy the journey!

FROM THE BIBLE:

"Show me your ways, O Lord, teach me your paths; guide me in your truth and teach me, for you are God my Savior, and my hope is in you all day long."

PSALM 25: 4-5 (NIV)

DIRECTION FOR TODAY:

How have you found your career path? Are you confident that you are now on the perfect path?

_____

_____

_____

_____

_____

_____

_____

THE MASTER MIND PRINCIPLE

HERE'S A POWERFUL SOURCE OF INSIGHT, UNDERSTANDING AND ABILITY TO ACCOMPLISH YOUR GOALS.

One of the most powerful groups I have ever been connected with has been a reading/study group that we call The Eagles Club. What we have seen in idea development and personal growth has been nothing short of astounding. In Napoleon Hill's timeless classic *"Think and Grow Rich"* he talks about Andrew Carnegie's Secret of Success. Carnegie had a Master Mind group by which he surrounded himself with the advice, counsel, and personal cooperation of other businessmen.

The "Master Mind" is defined as: *"coordination of knowledge and effort, in a spirit of harmony, between two or more people for the attainment of a definite purpose."* Hill further adds, *"No two minds ever come together without, thereby, creating a third invisible, intangible force which may be likened to a third mind."*

A friend is someone who knows the song in your heart, and sings it back to you when you have forgotten how it goes.

The Eagles Club is eleven guys who have been meeting together each Wednesday morning for several years. We select great books in advance and we each take turns leading the discussion. But the real power is not in learning new information as much as it is in relating to each other's lives in ways that people seldom experience. We read together, share personal applications, pray for each other, and are available at any time for help or counsel.

"The glory of friendship is not in the outstretched hand, nor the kindly smile, nor the joy of companionship; it is in the spiritual inspiration that comes to one when he discovers that someone else believes in him and is willing to trust him."
—**Ralph Waldo Emerson**

I see many people struggling to develop an idea, a business, or just their personal growth without taking advantage of this principle. I have always been fascinated with the concept of "synergy." That phenomenon whereby the total equals more than the sum of the parts (e.g. 1+1=3). This may not hold water with the mathematicians but conceptually it does make sense. We are told that one Belgian horse can pull about 8,000 lbs. So we would think logically that two Belgian horses in a yoke could pull about 16,000 lbs. But the truth is that together they can pull about 25,000 lbs and with a little training they will go to nearly 32,000 lbs. That's twice what we could mathematically expect. But that's the incredible power of the Master Mind principle.

FROM THE BIBLE:

"I appeal to you, brothers, in the name of our Lord Jesus Christ, that all of you agree with one another so that there may be no divisions among you and that you may be perfectly united in mind and thought."

I CORINTHIANS 1:10 (NIV)

DIRECTION FOR TODAY:

Who is in your Master Mind group? Who would you like to have in one? What can you do to initiate that?

_____

_____

_____

_____

_____

BUT THE PAY IS GOOD

IS MONEY THE ONLY REASON YOU GO TO WORK EACH DAY?

One of the questions on my information form for clients asks him/her to briefly describe their current work situation: *"Intolerable, evil, degrading, dirty, back-breaking, dehumanizing, demoralizing, but the pay is good."* This was the written response from a lady who was thinking about making a change. She had been with a government agency for 9 years and really was paid quite well. However, she like many of us, came to the realization that money is ultimately never enough compensation for investing our time and energy. There must be a sense of meaning, accomplishment and purpose.

Carl Jung, the psychoanalyst, said we go through seasons in our lives. In the first seasons, we are more concerned with physical and material needs—food on the table, a roof over our heads, etc. But as we approach the mid-life seasons we all start to ask questions that are more philosophical and spiritual—*Is there really a purpose for my life? Am I making a difference? How will I be remembered?* These questions require different kinds of answers. Fortunately, there does not have to be a trade-off. Doing something that is "noble" or something that makes a difference does not have to mean that we will lower our income. In fact, what I usually see is that when there is an authentic alignment of how God has gifted us, more money comes our way. Knowing that money is a by-product of doing something we love and doing it with excellence, it should come as no surprise that it's harder to make money doing something we don't enjoy. Finding our purpose or mission in life not only brings a sense of fulfillment and accomplishment, it releases a feeling of self-confidence, boldness, enthusiasm and money.

Jung says, *"The primary concerns of the first half are biological and social, while those of the second are cultural and spiritual. Man has two aims, the first is the natural aim, the begetting of children and the business of protecting the brood; to this belongs the acquisition of money and social position. Only when this aim has been achieved does the new aim — the cultural aim — become feasible.*

Success in the first half of life usually requires channeling one's energies single-mindedly in a specific direction. This results in development of a relatively narrow, one-sided personality and a failure to actualize much self-potential which remains dormant in the unconscious. The crisis of mid-life can serve to 'wake up' this dreaming undiscovered Self and the rest of life can provide the opportunity for its development." Carl Jung

If the pay is the only thing keeping you in your job, you are likely sacrificing your health, your confidence, your enthusiasm, a higher level of income and the authenticity to fully be what God created you to be.

FROM THE BIBLE:

"But those who want to be rich fall into temptation, a trap, and many foolish and harmful desires, which plunge people into ruin and destruction."

I TIMOTHY 6: 9 (HCSB)

DIRECTION FOR TODAY:

Have you been able to "wake up" the more important part of who you are? What are you doing to give expression to your "noble" self?

_____

_____

_____

_____

_____

_____

_____

_____

BOY, DO I FEEL CRABBY

WE HAVE THE ABILITY TO CHOOSE OUR ATTITUDES AND OUR HAPPINESS FOR TODAY.

I frequently draw from the wisdom of the Peanuts comic strip. In one episode, Lucy announces, *"Boy, do I feel crabby!"*

Her little brother Linus, is quick to try to rescue his sister. *"Maybe I can be of help. Why don't you just take my place here in front of the TV while I go and fix you a nice snack? Sometimes we all need a little pampering to help us feel better."* Then Linus brings her a sandwich, a few chocolate chip cookies, and some milk.

"Now is there anything else I can get you?" he asks. *"Is there anything I haven't thought of?"*

"Yes there's one thing you haven't thought of," Lucy responds. And then she screams in his direction, *"I don't want to feel better!"*

> **"The greater part of our happiness or misery depends on our dispositions, and not on our circumstances."** — **Martha Washington**

Lucy exemplifies a characteristic I see in a lot of people. They don't really want to change. Bad attitudes, bad decisions, bad habits and bad results just seem to be too comfortable to risk any substantial change. We all have things in our histories that we cannot change. We can't change our nationality, our parents or the health we had yesterday — But we all have the ability to change our thinking and our attitudes today. And those will impact our results tomorrow.

> **"I don't sing because I'm happy; I'm happy because I sing."** — **William James**

In his book *"Today Matters"* John Maxwell tells the story of a 92-yr-old lady who was moving into a nursing home. As she was being wheeled down the corridor to her new room, the attendant began to describe the room. *"I love it,"* the old women enthused. *"But you haven't even seen the room yet,"* the attendant reminded her. *"That doesn't have anything to do with it,"* she replied. *"Happiness is something you decide on ahead of time. Whether I like my room or not doesn't depend on how the furniture is arranged. It's how I arrange my mind."*

What an incredible opportunity—to arrange our mind in advance; to decide whether we are going to be happy or crabby!

FROM THE BIBLE:

"A gentle answer turns away wrath, but a harsh word stirs up anger. The tongue of the wise commends knowledge, but the mouth of the fool gushes folly. The eyes of the Lord are everywhere, keeping watch on the wicked and the good. The tongue that brings healing is a tree of life, but a deceitful tongue crushes the spirit."

PROVERBS 15: 1-4 (NIV)

DIRECTION FOR TODAY:

What attitude have you chosen for today? Have you decided to be happy or crabby?

_____

_____

_____

_____

_____

_____

THE MAGIC PEBBLES

THE GREATEST LIFE LESSONS ARE USUALLY NOT OBVIOUS IN ADVANCE.

One night a group of nomads were preparing to retire for the night when suddenly they were surrounded by a bold, bright light. They knew they were in the presence of God. With great anticipation, they awaited a heavenly message of great importance that they knew must be especially for them.

> *"The universe is full of magical things, patiently waiting for our wits to grow sharper."*
> **—Eden Phillips**

Finally the voice spoke. *"Gather as many pebbles as you can. Put them in your saddlebags. Travel a day's journey and tomorrow night will find you glad and it will find you sad."* After the heavenly spirit departed, the nomads shared their disappointment and anger with each other. They expected the revelation of great universal truth. Instead, they were given a menial task that made no sense to them at all. However, the memory of the brilliance of their visitor caused each one to pick up a few pebbles and deposit them in their saddlebags while voicing their displeasure.

They traveled a day's journey and the next night while making camp, they reached into their saddlebags and discovered every pebble they had gathered had become a diamond. They were glad they had diamonds. They were sad they had not gathered more pebbles.

> *"And now here is my secret, a very simple secret; it is only with the heart that one can see properly; what is essential is invisible to the eye."*
> **—Antoine de Saint-Exupery**

In 1988 I suffered a devastating business crash. Banking relationships changed and the aftermath of that forced me to liquidate a business at public auction. The resulting debts seemed overwhelming and did require twelve long years to get back to zero. However, in that process I learned some new ways to operate a business. Today my business runs with no bank debt and none of the other high fixed overhead processes I thought were necessary parts of any business. I am able to very profitably teach, speak and write on the transition we have seen from *production work* to *knowledge work* and the opportunities inherent in that change. I have time control and freedom that I never anticipated were possible.

> *"A man of character finds a special attractiveness in difficulty, since it is only by coming to grips with difficulty that he can realize his potentialities."*
> **—Charles De Gaulle**

Sometimes life's lessons are not obvious in advance. Trust that God's plan and your success is a process. Enjoy the journey of each day.

FROM THE BIBLE:

"And trusting means looking forward to getting something we don't yet have—for a man who already has something doesn't need to hope and trust that he will get it. But if we must keep trusting God for something that hasn't happened yet, it teaches us to wait patiently and confidently."

ROMANS 8:24-25 (TLB)

DIRECTION FOR TODAY:

What is a possible lesson you are learning right now?

_____

_____

_____

_____

_____

MASTER GARDENER OF YOUR SOUL

OUR MINDS ARE LIKE GARDENS; THEY GROW WHATEVER WE ALLOW TO TAKE ROOT.

"Just as a gardener cultivates his plot, keeping it free from weeds, and growing the flowers and fruits, which he requires, so may a man tend the garden of his mind, weeding out all the wrong, useless, and impure thoughts, and cultivating toward perfection the flowers and fruits of right, useful, and pure thoughts. By pursuing this process, a man sooner or later discovers that he is the master gardener of his soul, the director of his life. He also reveals, within himself, the laws of thought, and understands, with ever-increasing accuracy, how the thought-forces and mind-elements operate in the shaping of his character, circumstances, and destiny." From *"As a Man Thinketh"* by James Allen

"The thoughts we choose to think are the tools we use to paint the canvas of our lives."
— **Louise Hay**

When our children were young, we chose to eliminate the TV from our home. Of course they were devastated at being "deprived" of this basic human provision. All the neighborhood kids got to spend unlimited time watching MTV and the other popular shows of the day. However, over a short period of time it became obvious that our home was the most popular gathering place in the neighborhood. We played games, created sports events, and actually talked to each other. We also emphasized to our children that our minds are like computers. They process what we put into them. Yes, our children grew tired of hearing my clichés like *"garbage in, garbage out."* But we confirmed the principle of putting positive, pure thoughts into our minds as a prerequisite of getting positive, clean, productive results. Today all three of our children are avid readers and learners. They have a wealth of knowledge about specific areas of interest and have developed unique areas of specialty.

"I find television very educating. Every time somebody turns on the set, I go into the other room and read a book."

—**Groucho Marx**

I often tell people that if you read approximately 20 minutes a day you will complete one book per month. That's twelve new books a year. We are told that you can be an expert on any topic if you will read three books on that subject. Do you see how easy it is to set yourself apart from the average person? The mind is one of God's most amazing gifts to man. Scientists tell us we use approximately 2 percent of the brain power available to us

A room without books is like a body without a soul.

—**G. K. Chesterton (1874 - 1936)**

Control your own destiny by controlling what goes into your mind. The books you read, the thoughts you think, the TV you watch, the conversations you participate in, the people you associate with, and the music you listen to combine to create your future. Are you sowing the seeds for the life you want five years from now?

FROM THE BIBLE:

"Finally, brothers, whatever is true, whatever is noble, whatever is right; whatever is pure, whatever is lovely, whatever is admirable—if anything is excellent or praiseworthy—think about such things."

PHILIPPIANS 4: 8 (NIV)

DIRECTION FOR TODAY:

What seeds are you going to plant in your mind today?

_____

_____

_____

Do You Need a Small Fire in Your Life

PROTECTING THE STATUS QUO MAY BE PREVENTING YOU
FROM MORE FULFILLING OPPORTUNITIES.

According to the science of complexity, when a living system is in a state of equilibrium, it is less responsive to change. Prolonged sameness can therefore leave a system vulnerable and open to major disaster.

An example in nature would be the absolute prevention of forest fires. To keep the parks open to visitors, we see a constant emphasis on fire prevention. But fires are a natural part of the cycle of regeneration and cleansing for that system. Preventing even small fires allows a buildup of the undergrowth so that when a fire does occur, rather than just cleaning out the ground cover, it destroys even the tall mature trees. In recent years, we have seen the stories of raging fires, consuming valuable trees, expensive homes, and businesses as they are fueled by years of undergrowth.

If we don't change our direction we're likely to end up where we're headed.
—Chinese Proverb

Is the sameness and constancy in your life a blessing or is it leaving you vulnerable? Is 20 years on the same job a sign of great loyalty or has it made you complacent and unaware of the changes that have occurred in the workplace? Do you resist change at all costs?

You are not here merely to make a living. You are here to enable the world to live more amply, with greater vision, and with a finer spirit of hope and achievement. You are here to enrich the world. You impoverish yourself if you forget this errand.

—Woodrow Wilson (1856 - 1924)

Following a presentation in a church on *"living out your dreams"* I had a gentleman immediately push to approach me. He described having no dreams, no goals, and no vision for the future. This was frustrating to him and he wondered why he was missing those elements I had listed as expected components of anyone's daily existence. He went on to describe a long professional life in a respected position in the community. However, the predictable sameness of his life had in fact crowded out his dreams, goals and vision. We've heard the adage that the good is the enemy of the best. This is an example of that phenomenon. Reasonable success can blur the necessity of seeking out the best.

Blaze with the fire that is never extinguished.
—**Luisa Sigea, O Magazine, September 2003**

It's important to allow for flexibility. Keeping too rigid in our lives can restrict natural growth and positive change, making any unexpected change turn into a major disaster. For any system to survive and grow it must be capable of welcoming variety within its system. Maybe you need to give up the plaid sport coat and trade in the AMC Pacer. You may need to actually light a little fire in your life today!

FROM THE BIBLE:

"Where there is no vision, the people perish."

PROVERBS 29: 18 (KJV)

DIRECTION FOR TODAY:

Where do you need to start a fire in your life today?

_____

_____

_____

_____

_____

- **Need a change in your work life? Make the decision now to create the change you want in the next 48 Days.** You may be asking, why *48 Days*? Well, the Bible is very clear that God considers "40 days" to be a spiritually significant time period. In fact, in the Bible, any time God wanted to prepare people for something better, He took 40 days. Surely you can do something significant in 48 Days.
- **Check out all of Dan Miller's 48 Days Products** – Career Tools – Articles – Personality Profiles – Free Newsletter – Up-to-date Workplace News and more at: www.48Days.com

Fax Orders: 615-599-9620

Telephone Orders: 800-373-7771

Email Orders: info@48Days.com

Postal Orders: Vitology Press, P.O. Box 116, Arrington, TN 37014

The next *48 Days* can transform your life. I'm absolutely confident of that. No matter where you see yourself starting, *48 Days* is adequate time to look at how you are uniquely gifted, identify your strongest characteristics, consider the options, choose the best path for meaningful and fulfilling work, create a plan of action and ACT.

Believing that God created me for His purposes and is the ultimate "rudder of the day," I commit the next 48 Days to a new clarity and a plan of action for moving into God's "calling" for me.

_____

_____   _____
Name   Date

Register for FREE weekly tips at: www.48Days.com